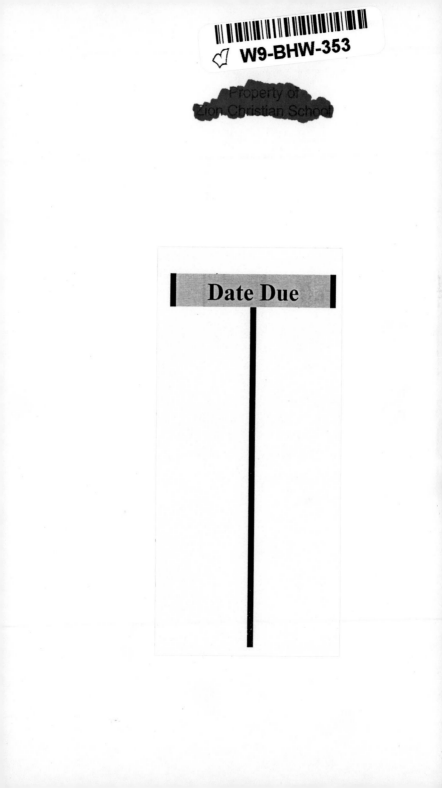

Date Due

CHRISTOPHER COLUMBUS
Discoverer of America

Christopher Columbus' greatest discovery was not the New World. As a young boy Columbus trusted Christ as his Saviour and discovered the ways of God. This little-known fact was the reason for his adventurous life.

Columbus felt God wanted him to explore the world and find new land and people so that Christ could be proclaimed. Finding boats and money to make the trip turned into a grueling experience in discouragement. Kings and queens promised and failed him. But Columbus was determined. He had promised God!

Growing up in Italy was exciting. Shipwreck, pirates, and storms marred his early sailing career. But he became an excellent sailor and businessman.

Columbus overcame all problems with God's help even mutiny and being bound with chains. See through his eyes the dangerous voyage to the New World as you read the words from his diary. Feel the excitement at sighting land and discovering gold. Weep with him over the massacre and troubles. Written as if Columbus is talking, walk beside him in his exciting adventures and let him tell you his unique story.

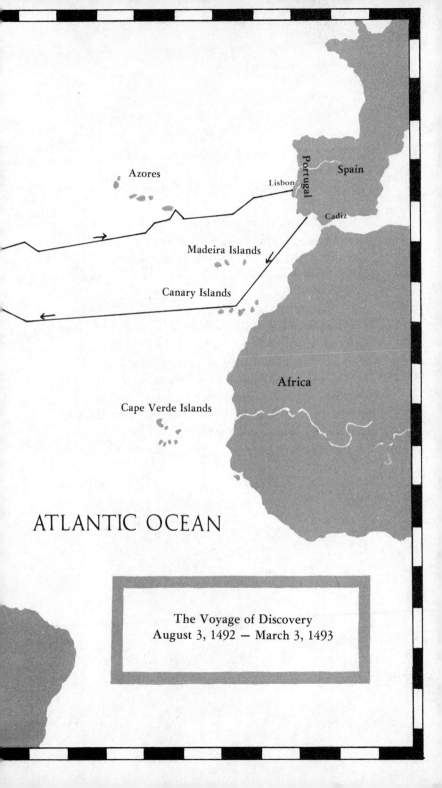

Azores

Portugal Spain

Lisbon

Cadiz

Madeira Islands

Canary Islands

Africa

Cape Verde Islands

ATLANTIC OCEAN

The Voyage of Discovery
August 3, 1492 – March 3, 1493

ABOUT THE AUTHOR

Bennie Rhodes is an evangelist and Christian writer. His writing talent has combined with his hobby of reading history and his Christian insight to produce a unique book on Christopher Columbus' spiritual life.

Mr. Rhodes is the author of numerous short stories, religious articles, and Sunday school curriculum materials for adults and children. He travels extensively holding evangelistic campaigns and Bible conferences. For eighteen years he served as a pastor in Georgia and Louisiana and for seven years taught Bible courses at Mercer Extension. Mr. Rhodes is a graduate of Mercer University, and New Orleans Theological Seminary. He resides in Georgia with his wife and two children.

ADVENTURER OF FAITH
AND COURAGE

CHRISTOPHER
COLUMBUS

Bennie Rhodes

ILLUSTRATED BY A. G. SMITH JR.

Property of
Zion Christian School

MOTT
MEDIA

Milford, Michigan 48042

To my faithful companion, Peggy,
who has encouraged me along the way
to sail a few uncharted seas myself.

Norma Cournow Camp, Editor

LIBRARY OF CONGRESS CATALOGING IN PUBLICATION DATA

Rhodes, Bennie, 1927-
    Christopher Columbus, Discoverer of America.

    (The Sowers)
    Bibliography: p. 144
    Includes index.

    SUMMARY: A biography of Christopher Columbus told in the first
person and emphasizing his desire from childhood to carry the Gospel of
Jesus Christ to new places.
    1. Colombo, Christoforo — Juvenile literature. [1. Columbus,
Christopher. 2. Explorers. 3. America — Discovery and exploration]
I. Title.

E111.R45   970'.01'50924 [B] [92]   76-5788
ISBN 0-915134-07-1 hardcover
ISBN 0-915134-26-8 paper

FOREWORD

Writing a book about Christopher Columbus, one of the truly great men in history, has been an exciting adventure. I could not have done so without the help of many others who have also been challenged to tell his story. I am indebted particularly to Samuel E. Morison and his excellent book *Admiral of the Ocean Sea*; to Bradford Ernle for his illustrated *Christopher Columbus*; and to Bjorn Landstrom for his work *Columbus*. I also relied heavily upon the biography of Columbus written by his son Ferdinand entitled *Life of the Admiral Christopher Columbus* and translated by Benjamin Keen; and upon the *Journal of Christopher Columbus*, written by Columbus himself on his first voyage, which provided some amazing insights into the Admiral's mind.

Since I have written the Admiral's story in the first person, it was necessary that some imaginative fiction be used. I have made an honest effort to imagine the things he would have thought and said in the course of the events which shaped his life.

Insofar as the names, major events, and places are concerned, they are all real, and I tried to tell the story just as it happened. In a few instances I have quoted Columbus' actual words from his journal. Since all of the story is in the first person these actual quotes have not been set apart in any special way (except in cases where I was quoting a letter or a document), but they are woven into the narrative.

There are some incidents where imagination was used to fill in unknown spots. The story of how Columbus met his wife, Felipa, is an example. Since no one knows how this actually occurred, it was necessary to invent some details at this point. This is true in other places, too. In the case of Columbus' conversations with his cabin boy, Pedro, some imaginative fiction was used. I felt, for instance, that since Columbus was a person who shared his innermost feelings with those closest to him, that he most surely would have discussed his personal faith in Jesus with his little friend. In all of these situations however, I have tried to imagine how these things could have happened, and have kept them as close to actual circumstances as possible.

This is also true of actual conversations and dialog recorded in the story. Obviously, no one can determine the actual words that were spoken, except in a few instances where they were recorded. So, most of the quoted conversations are products of my mind. I have tried to be as accurate as possible. If there are cases where accuracy fails, it is due to errors of the mind and not of the heart.

I wish to say a word of thanks to my wife who allowed me to "live" with Christopher Columbus for sometime, to my daughter, Leara, for her encouragement and help, and to my daughter-in-law, Sherryl, for her help in typing the manuscript. I am also deeply indebted to Mrs. Norma Camp for her invaluable criticism and help with revisions of the manuscript. Without these my task would have been much more difficult.

It is my hope and prayer that young readers will be inspired by the great man Columbus to become Christ-Bearers themselves in their own generation. If this could happen, the story I have told would truly be worth all the effort it took to tell it.

Bennie Rhodes
Griffin, Georgia
June 1975

CONTENTS

the ChRist-BeaReR

I was standing on the deck of the ship, watching the waves as they lapped against the side. I didn't even notice the big, burly seaman who nearly stumbled over me.

"What are you doing on this ship, boy?" he yelled. His eyes glared down from beneath big, bushy eyebrows.

"Well, I — I," I stammered, trying to think of what to say in my defense.

Another voice sounded, startling both of us. We turned to see the captain, a giant, hulking man, with a friendly face.

"What's your name, lad?" he asked.

"Christopher Columbus," I replied. "I'm the son of Domenico, the master weaver." I hoped that my father's reputation might spare me an embarrassing moment.

Whether the captain knew my father or not, he didn't say. He did treat me kindly though.

"All right, son," he said, "you can stay on board awhile. But stay out of the way. These men have gotta' work, you know."

I thanked him for his kindness. Then when he started to move away, I ran to him.

"May I sail with you, sir?" I asked, surprised at my own bravery.

The captain smiled, "How old are you lad?"

"I'm ten, captain. But I have sailed some with my father and my brother Bartholomew when we went to pull in the nets and —"

The captain interrupted. "I'm afraid you're a little too young, my boy. You come back when you're a few years older, and we'll see what we can do." With that the captain walked away and disappeared among the sailing rigs.

I was disappointed, but the promise that I could sail someday lifted my spirits. For a long time I walked around the deck, smelling the sea air, and feeling the pitch of the boat under my feet. I was careful to stay out of the way.

Suddenly, the command boomed, "Cast off!"

Before I could decide what to do a sailor yelled, "Get that boy off this boat!"

I ran to the edge of the deck and a big, husky sailor lifted me over the side. I fell to the dock panting with excitement and lay there watching the big ship glide quietly away. The sails were hoisted, gleaming in the sun. The ship receded further and further away.

I sat on the dock for a long time and watched the gleaming sails. The ship got smaller and smaller until it was only a speck on the horizon. The ship seemed to disappear over a curve. I wondered to myself, "Could the world really be round?" as I had read in a book about geography. It certainly seemed as though the ship had gone over the top and disappeared.

"One day I will find out," I said. I dreamed about sailing to far away lands, to places where men had never been before. "Someday, I will find out for myself what the world is really like. And when I do I will be the captain of a ship, perhaps even an admiral!"

That sounded good. "Christopher Columbus, Admiral of the Ocean Sea." With a title like that all the world would know that I was born to sail the seas.

While dreaming, I heard someone call. "Chris! Chris!" yelled my younger brother, Bartholomew. "You'd better come home. Supper is almost ready, and Father won't like it if he knows you're hanging around the docks again."

I liked my brother Bartholomew. He was always kidding me about my red hair, which he said was shocking, and my rugged complexion, which he described as the look of a seaman.

Walking home that day, we talked of the ships that sailed from our city of Genoa, Italy. We were proud to be growing up in a city that sent ships out to many of the great ports of the world. We both dreamed that someday we would sail together, perhaps through uncharted seas to strange lands in faraway places.

Our mother, Susanna, had prepared supper. My father joined us for the meal. I was glad he did not ask me where I had been that day. Of course, Bartholomew would not tell unless Father asked him.

Father was excited that night about a meeting of the weaver's guild which had been called to discuss the problems of obtaining wool. Since 1453, two years after I was born, Genoa's woolen trade with Constantinople had been almost completely cut off as a result of the war between the Ottoman Turks and the Christians. The Turks had overrun the city of Constantinople, stopping trade with cities in the Mediterranean.

My father and the other weavers of Genoa were

forced to look elsewhere for wool supplies. Father had been out of wool for several days now, and the situation for him was getting desperate. I felt some pangs of guilt and cast a glance at Bartholomew. He and I had been glad at first that Father was out of wool. We enjoyed having a few days off from our jobs in the shop. But we realized now that unless our father got wool soon there would be no money for food. I prayed secretly that things would be worked out at the meeting, even though I dreaded going back to work.

Bartholomew and I worked in father's shop carding the raw wool so that mother, and another weaver, could weave the wool into cloth. Carding was a slow process of separating the wool fibers and lining them up in parallel rows for the weaver. It was hard work and sometimes we worked long hours at our tasks.

But on this night we all relaxed. It would be several days before we would have any wool to card and meanwhile the ships would be sailing. There would be plenty of time to slip away to the docks again.

"Hurry up with your supper, boys. You know we must go to church tonight." This time it was Mother who was excited. I had forgotten what day this was!

"Yes," Father said. "That's right. Today is Christopher's birthday." He slid a small coin across the table. I really did not want to accept it, but my mother looked at me, and I knew I'd better. She sensed what I was thinking, though. Times were hard and I knew Father did not have any coins to spare. But I took the coin. It was the custom.

I do not really know on what day I was born. In Genoa we celebrated our birthdays on the feast day of our patron saint. My patron saint was Saint

Christopher, and that day, June 25, was the feast day of Saint Christopher, a very important date for me.

After supper we made our way through the cobbled streets to a tiny church. There, in the semi-darkness we sat and listened once again to the legend of Saint Christopher. I already knew every detail of the old tale, but I listened once more, and dreamed a little about the ships.

Christopher, in whose honor I was named, was a giant Syrian who lived not long after my Saviour. He was converted to the Christian faith by an old hermit who spoke to him one day about becoming a Christian.

"Perhaps our Lord will show Himself to you if you fast and pray," the hermit told Christopher.

"Fast I cannot," said Christopher, "and how to pray I know not; ask me something easier."

"Knowest thou that river without a bridge which can only be crossed at great peril of drowning?" asked the hermit.

"I do," replied Christopher.

"Very well," continued the hermit, "do thou who art so tall and strong take up thine abode by the hither bank, and assist poor travelers to cross; that will be very agreeable to Our Lord, and mayhap He will show Himself to thee."

Christopher followed the advice of his hermit friend. He built himself a cabin near the river, and using a giant tree trunk as a staff, carried travelers across the stream on his broad shoulders.

One night while Christopher was asleep in his cabin he heard the voice of a child in the darkness.

"Christopher! Come and set me across," the Child pleaded.

The big giant came stalking out the cabin with a staff in his hand and set the Child on his shoulders. Out into the stream he went. But as he traveled, the Child's weight increased so that it became almost unbearable, even for a giant. Christopher was forced to call forth every ounce of strength he had in his tremendous body to make it to the other side. After he had struggled for some time and made it to the distant shore, he set the Child down safely.

"Well now, my little fellow," said Christopher, "thou has put me in great danger, for thy burden waxed so great that had I borne the whole world on my back, it could have weighed no more than thou."

"Marvel not, Christopher," the Child said, "for thou hast borne upon thy back the whole world and Him who created it. I am the Christ whom thou servest in doing good; and as proof of my words, plant that staff near thy cabin, and tomorrow it shall be covered with flowers and fruit."

Christopher followed the instructions of the Child and the next day his staff had turned into a beautiful date palm, which provided food and shade for the saint.

Bartholomew nudged me awake at this point in the story. I was glad because the next words became very real to me.

"And that is why Christopher came to be called the Christ-Bearer." As I perked up, he continued. "Perhaps some of us could become Christ-Bearers in our own day, bearing the Gospel to those who do not know our Blessed Lord."

I do not know what happened during the rest of the service. I was thinking of my name — Christopher Columbus, the Christ-Bearer. Could it be that God had ordained me to take His Gospel to heathen lands by way of the ships which I loved so much? Could Christopher Columbus, the Admiral of the Ocean Sea, take the news of my Saviour to strange, faraway lands?

I dreamed of the day when I might become a missionary for my Lord. In my Bible at home I had read from the pages of Zechariah how the Lord had promised that "he shall speak peace unto the heathen: and his dominion shall be from sea even to sea, and from the river even to the ends of the earth" (Zechariah 9:10).

When we knelt to pray I asked my Heavenly Father to allow me to become a Christ-Bearer, too. I asked Him to let me sail the seas and take the Christ Child to lands where His name and the message of salvation had never been heard. Sweet peace came into my soul that night for I knew that God had heard my prayer.

At home we were surprised to find Father and two men from the guild still arguing about the merits of buying wool from the Portuguese. Bartholomew and I sat on the floor in the corner and listened.

"We don't have any choice," argued my father. "The ships cannot trade any longer with Constantinople."

"Perhaps one day soon," one of the men spoke up, "we'll find another route to the Indies."

"Yes," my father replied. "One day soon. How soon? It may be years before trade with the Indies can be resumed."

"Domenico is right," replied the other man. "I think we had better recommend to the guild that we accept the offer from the Portuguese."

"All right, then," the first man agreed. "I suppose so. But meanwhile, let's pray that somebody will find a way to reopen our trade routes with the East." With these words the meeting broke up, and the men left for their homes.

"Is it really bad, Father?" I asked as we lingered.

"It's bad," he said. But realizing perhaps that our minds should not be bothered with such troubles, he said cheerfully, "We will have some wool in a few days. Then you boys can go back to work."

Bartholomew grunted and I chuckled under my breath. "We don't want any special favors, Father," we were saying quietly. "We're just not all that anxious to go back to work." But Father didn't hear us. He was too busy thinking about the new business deal he had made that day for wool.

"Time for bed, boys," Mother's voice rang out.

We jumped up and raced to the other room. Bartholomew got there first and was already kneeling for his prayers when I arrived. I knelt beside him and we prayed silently. Finally, Bartholomew stretched out on the pallet and watched me as I continued to pray. I must have prayed for a long time that night because when I finally got into bed beside my brother, he asked me, "What's bothering you, Chris?"

"Can you keep a secret?" I asked.

"Sure, I can," said Bartholomew. I knew he would, too.

"I don't want to be a weaver like Father," I whispered. "I want to be a sailor who sails the open seas and takes the Gospel to the heathen."

"Chris," he said, "do you really want to do that?"

"I want to do that more than anything else in the world," I replied with confidence.

"Well, Chris," said my brother. "If you really want to bad enough, I don't think anybody in the world can stop you. Only —"

"Only what?" I asked.

"What about me?" Bartholomew asked. "I don't want you to leave me."

"Oh, it will be awhile yet," I assured him. "Besides, I plan on taking you with me — if you want to go."

This excited Bartholomew so much that he

raised up off the pallet and stared at me in the
darkness. "Oh, Chris!" he whispered loudly.
"Would you really? I do want to go with you!"

"We'll go, Bart," I replied. "Someday you and I
will sail together. We'll ride the seas, and the
islands and the continents will rise up to meet us!"

We heard our father stirring in the next room.
Deciding that we had better be quiet, we lay there
in the darkness, dreaming our dreams. It had been
an exciting day. I settled down to get some sleep,
dreaming of Saint Christopher and the Christ
Child. As I dreamed, the ships in the harbor at
Genoa glistened in the moonlight waiting for
another day. Perhaps tomorrow I would be there
to watch them sail away.

BATTLE AT SEA

Sailing became the most important part of my life during the next few years. Bartholomew was my constant companion. We still worked in Father's shop during the winter months when the Mediterranean was filled with squalls and high winds which made it difficult to sail.

But when the weather permitted, we sailed. Most of our time was spent on a small sailing rig which Father leased from a merchant of Genoa. Bart and I took the finished wool from the shop and sailed up and down the coasts, to the small towns and villages that lay stretched out along the coastline of Italy. We traded the wool for cheese and wine and other things which we could sell for a profit.

On one of the sailing trips we encountered our first storm at sea. Bartholomew kept watching the little cloud which had formed to our left.

"I think there's a storm brewing over there," he pointed. Worry creased his forehead. The wind had picked up. The little sailing rig was tossing to and fro on the waves. I quickly set the sails to the

leeward side, hoping we would not be dashed
onto the shore. Just as we rounded a rocky cove
the storm broke heavily upon us. Waves slapped
the sides and spilled into the boat. The tiny rig
pitched and tossed on the angry waves while Bart
and I fought desperately to bring the sails in. The
ropes dug into our hands, and sea water stung our
eyes.

For the first time in my life I was afraid of the
sea. I looked at Bart and sensed that he was afraid,
too. He grimaced as he strained heavily with the
sails. The little rig pitched forward, throwing both
of us to our knees. I managed to regain my footing
just as a giant wave crashed into the boat sending
both of us reeling. Even our bones felt wet.

"Hold on, Bart!" I yelled. Bart was hanging
dangerously over the side, his feet dangling in the
air. He clung to the side of the boat with all his
strength. I grabbed on to his shoulders. The boat
pitched and swayed. I thought any moment we
were going under as wave after wave pounded the
sides. Bart held on though. At last I was able to
heave him aboard. He lay stretched out, panting
and sobbing in the two inches of water in the
bottom of the boat.

Finally, we managed to slip the rig into a cove
and tossed out the anchors. Huddling in the tiny
rig, drenched with heavy rains, we rode out the
storm.

When the sea was calm, Bart and I knelt in the
rig and thanked God for sparing our lives. We
knew our Saviour had been with us through the
storm.

Although my father, Domenico, was a respected businessman, he sometimes had to struggle to
make ends meet. I did not realize it at the time, but
I learned later that he was a dreamer like me. I
dreamed of sailing the ocean seas, but my father

dreamed of getting rich. But for some reason or other, his schemes for getting wealth never worked. Instead, we seemed to get poorer and poorer as the years rolled on.

One day when I was fourteen, I came home from the docks to supper. The table was bare except for a few pieces of cheese. Mother poured the last bit of milk for my sister Bianca and my little brother Giovanni. Father's business fortunes were at the lowest ebb we had ever seen.

While sitting at the table, I finally got up the nerve to tell my family an important bit of news.

"There's a ship going out to Chios tomorrow," I said. "I'm going to sail with her. The captain has already hired me."

My mother cried softly. "Domenico," she pleaded, "do not let him go. He is too young to be going to sea."

"But, Mother," I exclaimed, "I can earn the wages of a man! Besides, I'll only be gone for a few weeks."

I reached in my pocket and pulled out the coins which the good captain, Nicolo, had paid in advance. I placed them in Mother's hands. She gasped at the size of the coins.

Father had not said a word. Finally, he spoke. "It may be a good thing for Christopher to sail. After all he is growing up and needs to see the world."

"But what about me?" cried Bartholomew. In all the excitement he had been forgotten. I reached over and touched my brother's shoulder.

"I'll be back soon," I said. "And someday you and I will sail together. But right now you must stay here and help Father card the wool."

So, I sailed on my first galleass. It was a big ship for those days with a crew of about thirty men. The captain, Nicolo Spinolo, was a kind man who taught me many things about sailing. I think he recognized, even on that first voyage, that I was destined to be a sailor.

Our destination was Chios, a Greek island in the Aegean Sea. I will always remember those warm, balmy days in the Straits of Messina, passing quietly by Scylla and Charybdis. Then on we sailed through the channel behind Cythera where we sighted the white columns of the Temple of Poseidon in the distance.

One day when I was learning to tend the compass beside the ship's mate, Captain Spinolo came below to have a look.

"How are you doing, lad?" he asked, as he stepped over ropes near us.

"Fine, sir. Diego is showing me how to read the compass."

"Very good," replied the captain. "Perhaps when you have finished you would like to look over the charts with me."

"I would like that very much," I said. "May I come now, sir?"

"Yes," said the captain. He looked at Diego and winked. "I suppose Diego can manage the compass without you."

I hustled alongside the captain until we reached the cabin built on the forecastle of the galleass. The tiny room had a table by the window and a couple of stools. A pallet on the floor for the captain was a luxury item which we ordinary seamen did not enjoy. We slept on the decks, or on the floor in the hold below with the cargo.

The charts were spread out on the table. For the first time in my life I saw the maps which guided the seamen in their sailing. I was fascinated as the captain pointed to the exact position of our ship at the moment. I noted the lines indicating wind currents and decided that someday I would make charts of my own. Only I wanted my charts to depict seas where sailors had never sailed before.

On Chios we picked up our precious cargo. Mostly it was mastic, which grew only on that island and was used as medicine throughout Europe. Genoese merchants controlled the island of Chios for centuries. The mastic from the lentish trees had made some of them very wealthy.

I cared little for the cargo, however. I was thrilled by the sailing and glad when the ship was finally loaded and we were out in the seas again. I loved to feel the wind and sun on my back, the gentle movement of the ship under my feet. I would stand on the forward deck and breathe the fresh air while the sea sent a soft, misty spray to refresh my face.

I worked beside the husky, experienced seamen. They taught me many things, including how to estimate distances by the eye, how to let go and weigh anchors, and how to set the sails to reap the greatest benefit from the prevailing winds.

The voyage finally ended as we dropped anchors in the harbor at Genoa. When I stepped off the ship, I realized how glad I was to be home again. It was good to see familiar faces, to walk the cobbled streets of the town where I was born. I felt like a man of the world who had been to faraway places and returned home as a conquering hero.

My family was glad to see me, too — especially when I brought the rest of my wages. We had a celebration that evening with food for everyone and plenty of milk for Bianca and Giovanni.

Bartholomew was pleased to see me, also. This was the longest time we had ever been separated, and he had missed his red-haired brother with the ruddy complexion very much.

At seventeen, I signed on a ship for the first time

as a trader. One of my father's business acquaintances had noticed how I had traded my father's wool for a profit. He asked if I would sail with a captain bound for the eastern ports of the Mediterranean.

I gladly accepted the position. We loaded the ship in Genoa with woolen goods (some from my father's shop too), cheese, and wine, and sailed away on the blue waters of the sea.

As a businessman aboard the ship, I had certain privileges I had never had before as an ordinary seaman. One of these was spending long hours with the captain, poring over the maps and charts and deciding in which ports we would trade.

During the trip the seamen told me about their strange adventures on their journeys to far off places.

One day a seaman showed me a map drawn by the ancient geographer, Ptolemy. "You can see, Christopher," he explained to me, "the earth is not flat. The earth is round."

"Of course it is," I replied. "They're even teaching this in the universities now. Someday, everyone will know the truth about the shape of the earth."

I noticed on the map which my friend showed me the ragged outlines of China and India. Between Europe and those great countries lay the vast expanse of the Atlantic Ocean.

"Why hasn't someone crossed that ocean?" I asked my seaman friend.

"Oh, Chris, my lad," he mused, "some have tried. But I guess they dropped off when they got to the end of the world." He chuckled when he said this because he did not believe it any more than I did. I determined then someday to sail in the great Atlantic Ocean.

When I returned home from that business trip, I

was full of exciting news about plans to sail in the Atlantic. My family had some exciting news, too.

First, I discovered that in my absence a new baby brother had been born. His name was Diego. Bart and I discussed his future that night.

"I would like to see that Diego gets an education," I said proudly, as the older brother.

"I would, too," said Bart. "I believe he will grow up to be a minister of the Gospel."

"That's a wonderful idea," I exclaimed. "That would make Mother very proud to have a clergyman in the family."

Mother smiled and I knew she agreed.

I felt ashamed of myself because of my failure to live up to the vows I had made to God. I prayed that He might forgive me for my slackness and vowed that I would still become a Christ-Bearer for Him.

Bartholomew had some exciting news for me, too, but he waited until he could talk to me privately.

"Chris," he began, as we walked down the street after supper. "I have made an important decision while you were gone."

"What is it, Bart?" I asked, puzzled now at the secrecy.

"I have decided I want to be a mapmaker," he announced. "I have already been apprenticed to a mapmaker in Lisbon." He paused to let this bit of news sink in.

"But what about the shop? Father's business?" I asked.

"Oh, I plan to stay on until he can find someone else. But then I am leaving for Lisbon!"

That was exciting news, and my heart turned over again as I thought how we had planned to sail together. But Bartholomew had not taken to the sea as I had. Perhaps, map making would be best for him.

In 1476 the Mediterranean nations were at war one with the other. It was a very troubled age, and the ships on which I had been sailing were forced to cease their trading. It was too dangerous for a single ship to sail because it would be fair prey to pirate frigates on the sea.

In May of that year Genoa organized a big convoy of ships to deliver a load of Chian mastic to Lisbon, England, and France. Since Father had all the help he needed, I decided to sign on as a mate.

I said good-bye to my family. Bartholomew was already in Lisbon and had developed into a master mapmaker. My mother and father wept at my leaving because of the dangers of the war.

My ship was called the *Bechalla*. We sailed from Noli on May 31 and worked our way westward through the straits. For the first time in my life I sailed into the great Atlantic Ocean and thus began the fulfillment of a dream.

We were well on our way to Lisbon, the first port of call. The sea was calm. It was one of the balmy, summer days I had learned to love. The crew was tense, however. We were sailing in convoy for protection. We knew possible danger lay ahead. We had three galleasses and a big armed ship, which belonged to the Spinolos in Genoa, plus the smaller caravels.

Early that morning we were just off the port of Lagos in southern Portugal when I heard the sound of thunder — I thought at first. The captain sounded the alarm and all men rushed to their stations. It was cannons booming in the distance, not thunder. The hot cannon balls hissed as they splashed in the water near our ship.

"Hoist the sails," cried the captain.

"Heave to, now!" I yelled above the din of the

distant cannons. The sails unfurled. The caravel
lurched forward to join the others in battle.

Soon we were in the midst of the fight. As the
battle raged the ships fired, advanced and retreated. Hours passed, and my bones ached from the
weariness of hoisting the heavy balls to the cannons mounted on the deck. Shells whistled all
about us, the air was heavy with the odor of sweat
and gun powder. We worked desperately to keep
the rigging erect and the cannons firing.

Late in the afternoon, bone weary and tired, I
heard a splitting sound on the port side. The ship
lurched sideways throwing me to the deck. A
French frigate had rammed our ship!

Men bounded over the rail. French privateers
were swarming over our deck, their swords gleam-
ed in the afternoon sun. Sailors leaped to the defense of the ship. Moans mixed with the sound of
clashing swords. Men crashed over the sides.
Wounded sailors flailed about in the water, and
many sank to a grave among the shells.

I drew my sword and lunged at the nearest
Frenchman. He went down beneath me. I scram-
bled to keep my footing amid the twisting, groan-
ing bodies, and the blood that soaked the deck.

Two pirates grabbed me from behind and
shoved me against the rail. Rough, seaman's hands
closed on my neck as I struggled away. I was
breathless and dizzy from swirling across the deck
— half walking, half stumbling. Another pirate hit
me in the side with his flashing sword and the next
thing I knew, I was in the water.

Cannon balls had hit the ship, and she was sinking. Two other ships, including one of the French
frigates, were on fire. The percussion of the ex-
ploding cannons made such pressure in my ears
they ached. Great balls of fire skimmed across
the water near me. Sailors were all around in the

water, some screaming, all trying desperately to swim away from the blazing inferno of the sinking ships. Would I escape this scene of horror alive, I wondered.

I reached out in the darkness and found an oar from one of the ships. I clung to it desperately, realizing that I could not swim with my wound. I felt my side and saw in the light from the burning ships little patches of blood oozing out into the water. There was a gaping hole of torn skin. I felt weak and helpless as I paddled around and through the screaming forms and still bodies of men.

On the distant shore I saw tiny lights flickering. I knew my only hope for survival was to paddle in that direction. I whispered a prayer to my Saviour and set out in the darkness for the shore.

All night I paddled slowly toward those lights. There were times when I was so weak from exhaustion and pain that I almost gave up. But I remembered the vows I had made to God. Surely, I could not die now because I had not fulfilled my mission.

"I must live," I thought, "so that I can become a Christ-Bearer. There are so many things I want to do for God."

I feel sure that God protected me that night. Hundreds of men died in the battle and the sinking of the ships. Even though I was wounded, God had spared my life.

At dawn I was still struggling in the sea when kind Portuguese fishermen carried me safely to shore. They took me to one of their tiny cottages and worked on my ugly wound. I whispered, "Where are we?"

"You are near Lisbon," one of them replied.

"Wonderful," I answered weakly. "I must go

there at once! I have a brother and some friends in Lisbon."

"I'm afraid you'll have to wait," one of the fishermen shook his head sadly. "You're in no shape for travel."

He was right. I was weak from loss of blood. The pain of my wound sent sharp, shivering signals to my brain. The wound needed much time to heal. So, I laid down on the floor and rested, and dreamed of starting a new life in Lisbon.

the BIRth
of an Idea

For two weeks I lay on the floor of the fisherman's cabin, barely able to move. Finally, my fisherman friend came with his cart, loaded me inside, and carried me to Lisbon. The little cart jolted along the rocky roads and cobbled streets of the city until the pain from my wound was almost unbearable. At times I cried out softly when sharp jabs of pain surged through my side. After making several inquiries, he at last found Bartholomew's shop.

Bart came running into the street. I lay huddled in the cart. "Chris," he asked, "is that really you?"

"I'm afraid it is, dear Brother, and I need some help."

Bart carried me inside his living quarters directly behind his shop. He immediately sent for a doctor to dress my wound. Later that night when I was feeling better, I told Bart all about the battle and how I was wounded.

"Well, Chris," said Bart, "you are very lucky to be alive!"

"And very lucky to be here with my brother!" I added.

For several months while the wound was healing, I helped Bartholomew in his map making business. It was an exciting business. We talked to many seamen.

Lisbon, at that time, was the busiest seaport in the world. Ships were sailing out of her harbor every day. The men who sailed them wanted the latest maps and charts available. Bartholomew's business was booming.

Prince Henry, the noble navigator, had founded an academy of geography and navigation not far from Lisbon. Out of that school came great men of courage and wisdom who were determined to extend man's knowledge of the world. From the port at Lisbon they went out, sailing down the coast of Africa, or north to England and Iceland. Each time they returned with more news about the world.

When I was able to get about again, I spent much time on the docks talking with these seamen. Many times I was delivering maps and charts, ordered from by brother, to the captains of these vessels.

One day I walked into Bartholomew's shop and announced that I was going to Iceland. My brother sought to discourage me.

"I had hoped you would stay here with me and help in my map making business," he said.

"I would love to, Bart," I replied. "But I have grown restless and anxious for the sea again." Bartholomew knew by this time that I was never completely happy unless I was sailing.

I sailed that year to England, then on to Iceland, where the icy waters of the North Atlantic filled us sometimes with fear. I was amazed to find that England carried on much trade with Iceland, swapping their goods for valuable furs. In those cold regions of the world I met many strange people.

Some of the seamen told me tales of a land far beyond Iceland. It was here that Eric, a Norseman of the past, had sailed. He had sighted a land flowing with natural wheat grain and vineyards which he called *Vinland*.

Some of the natives of Iceland who talked to us through an interpreter also told us about mysterious islands to the west. They had heard many stories of ships that had sailed to these distant lands.

These stories were fascinating. Some of them were merely tales. But I was convinced that by sailing west one could find these lands. Perhaps one could visit even China and Japan by sailing west!

I returned to Lisbon full of excitement about these possibilities. Together with Bart I went over all the maps and charts I could find which might help.

"I'm convinced, Bart, that many lands exist which have not yet been reached in the Atlantic."

"But ships are going out every day," Bart protested. "Surely if there were lands there someone would know."

"How can they know?" I asked. "You draw the charts and maps. You know that the ships are only sailing north and south. No one is sailing west."

"Yes, that is true," said Bart, rubbing his chin.

Working with Bart in his shop again was interesting. The excitement of drawing charts for the seamen helped pass the long months of my stay in Lisbon.

Bart and I both were learning to speak Portuguese, as well as Spanish and Latin. These languages were necessary in our business.

We also read many books. The invention of the printing press had made it possible for people to have books. I decided to go into the book selling business. Actually, I was still in the map making business with my brother, but I also sold books.

Of course, I read the books before selling them. But one of the books which I kept and refused to sell was *The Travels of Marco Polo*. In that wonderful book the traveler described the wonderful kingdoms of China and Cipangu (Japan). I read the book many times until I had become very familiar with those lands. Marco Polo said that in Cipangu there were many cities where the houses were domed with gold. I marveled at that.

I wanted to visit these strange places and take the Gospel of Jesus Christ to the millions of people who lived there.

One day when staring out the tiny window of our shop and dreaming about the gold-domed houses of Cipangu, I saw two young ladies walking down the street.

"Look at this, Bart!" I exclaimed. My brother, who was busy with his maps, came over to look.

We watched as the young ladies passed our window. The one on the right was very beautiful. Her eyes met mine as she passed by.

"Who are they?" I asked Bart.

"Which one do you mean?" Bart replied.

"The one nearest to the window when they passed," I replied. "She is a lovely one."

"Yes," Bart mused. "She is, isn't she? I would think they are probably enrolled in the school just down the street."

"How can we find out?" I inquired. I was anxious to meet the young lady.

"I'll see what I can find out, Chris," my brother said. "But meanwhile, I've got work to do."

The next day Bart came in from a trip delivering maps. "I found out who your lovely lady is," he announced. "She is Felipa Perestrello. She is enrolled in school just two blocks from here!"

"What else?" I asked my brother, eager to learn all I could about the charming lady.

"Well," Bart teased, "I did find out that she is the daughter of Bartholomew Perestrello, a very prominent man who was once governor of Porto Santo. He is now deceased."

"And she is not married?" I asked.

"No, she is not married, Chris," my brother smiled. "And not likely to be either — at least not to a common seaman. Her brother is now the governor of Madeira. Her family is very rich."

"She will marry me," I said to my brother, confident of my ability to win her.

"But how will you meet her?" Bart asked in amazement.

"I'll find a way," I smiled. "Don't worry. I'll find a way."

The following Sunday Bartholomew and I prepared ourselves for church as usual. We attended church faithfully as our dear mother had instructed us during our childhood. We usually attended a little church several blocks from our shop where many of our sailor customers went. This morning, however, I shoved my brother in the opposite direction to another church, located next to the school.

Before he knew what was happening we were inside the church waiting for the service to begin. I looked about in the semi-darkness and finally spotted her. Sitting directly across the aisle from us was Felipa, and her friend. She smiled as I looked at her and my heart fluttered.

Bart had spotted her, too. "So that's why you wanted to come here."

I nodded and smiled.

Needless to say, I had a difficult time following the service that day. All I could think of was Felipa Perestrello. "What a beautiful name," I thought. "Perhaps she would like to change it to Felipa Columbus!"

From that day on we went to every service at the new church. We always sat in the same place, directly across from Felipa and our eyes always met. I learned that going to church was not only good for my spiritual life, but for finding a mate, too. I was confident that someday I would have a chance to speak to Felipa Perestrello.

That day came very soon and when it did, I was ready. We were on our way out of the church when Felipa, who was walking in front of us, dropped her purse. Quickly I came to her rescue, bending over and retrieving the purse from the floor. I bowed graciously before her and presented her with the purse.

"Thank you, *Don* — ?" Felipa obviously wanted my name.

"Columbus," I replied. "Christopher Columbus."

"Thank you, *Don* Columbus," she said very graciously.

"You are welcome." Before we could continue our conversation, the crowd was upon us. We were forced to move on toward the door. By the time Bart and I reached the exit, she was gone.

Several days passed in which I did not see Felipa. We were busy in the shop, and I hardly had time to think of her. I could still hear her voice, especially at night when I lay in bed and could not sleep.

I returned home one afternoon to find a note on the desk from Bart, who was out. The note read:

Chris

Don Bartholomew Perestrello wishes to purchase some books from you. He would like to see you at eight tonight in his study.

Bart

I was puzzled by the note. Bart had told me that Felipa's father was named Bartholomew Perestrello. But he was dead. Could this be a ghost? Or was my brother simply playing a joke on me?

I looked at the address on the note. I knew the street, but it was a great distance from the shop. I packed up a few books and left in plenty of time to arrive by eight o'clock.

Promptly at eight I knocked on the door of the house. The door was opened by a servant girl who ushered me into a large drawing room. There I was greeted warmly by Bartholomew Perestrello.

"Hello," he said. "You must be the bookseller."

"Yes," I answered. "I found your message and brought along a few of my books."

"Very good," he replied. "But first I would like you to meet my mother, *Dona* Perestrello, and my sister, Felipa."

I looked around as Felipa and her mother entered the room. Bowing graciously before them, I expressed my delight at knowing them. At least I had cleared up a mystery. Felipa's brother had the same name as his father.

Governor Perestrello explained that he wanted me to look over their library and to place there the books which would be helpful to Felipa in her studies.

"This may require several trips, sir," I explained. "As I receive the books, I will need to deliver them."

"That will be quite all right, young man." It was Felipa's mother who answered. "You may come here any time you wish."

That meant I would have many opportunities to see Felipa. What joy! I left that night feeling lighter than clouds and sure that someday Felipa would be mine.

Felipa and I were married in the little church where we had met, with Governor Perestrello, *Dona* Perestrello, and Bart in attendance. It was a simple wedding, but Felipa and I were very happy and very much in love.

Not long after we were married the governor asked us to move to the island of Madeira to live with my mother-in-law. I was growing a bit tired of the map making business. I did not like sitting in a cramped little room all day. In Madeira I would be able to move about and work in the business of trading. Besides, the map making business had fallen off. There was hardly enough work for both Bart and I to do.

In Madeira we settled down to build a home together. At night my mother-in-law would tell us fascinating stories of her husband, Felipa's father. She told us how her husband had introduced rabbits to the island to provide food for the natives. But the rabbits had multiplied so rapidly that they ate all the vegetation and stripped the island bare. It was not until the rabbits were killed off and the balance of nature was restored that things returned to normal.

We laughed about Bartholomew Perestrello and his rabbits.

But she also told us of her husband's interest in the sea. Especially did he believe that many islands existed that had not been found. One night my mother-in-law came in with an armful of maps and charts.

"These were my husband's," she said. "But, now, because you are interested in the sea, I want you to have them."

Felipa and I spent many hours looking at those charts.

"Look, Felipa," I said one day. "Your father drew many islands on these maps. I am convinced that there are many others and I want to find them."

Then I told Felipa about Marco Polo and the great lands of the East. I also showed her Ptolemy's map and explained that it was only a short hop across the Atlantic to these fantastic lands.

"How far do you think they are?" she asked.

"Not far," I replied. "Perhaps a month's journey."

"But you cannot go alone," Felipa insisted. "It is too dangerous."

"No," I said, "I will need at least three ships to carry men and supplies. But I can do it, Felipa. I can sail west and find the great lands of the East."

Felipa looked at me with tenderness in her eyes. "I know you want to go, Chris, and I believe you will someday. But I think you had better wait awhile."

"Why?" I asked without really thinking.

"Because you're going to be a father," she said. "You wouldn't want to be away when that happens, would you?"

I took Felipa in my arms and kissed her.

"No, Dear," I replied, "I wouldn't miss that for all the gold in Cipangu!"

In March of the following year I did become a father. Our little son was born. We named him Diego in honor of my brother in Genoa.

search for
a sponsor

A few months after Diego was born I became anxious to put my plan for sailing west to reach the Indies into action. I wrote a letter to Bartholomew in Lisbon outlining the plan. I told him to expect me soon for I hoped to present my plan to King John of Portugal.

My brother-in-law, the governor, made arrangements for me to be presented in King John's court by writing a letter of introduction for me. When he had done this, I sailed to Lisbon with Felipa and Diego, my son.

After I had carefully gone over the plans with Bartholomew, I presented myself to the king. The king greeted me as I entered his chambers and bowed. He was surrounded by a group of advisors who seemed to be anxious to hear of my plan to reach the Indies.

When I first stood before them I was tense and excited. My mouth was dry, and I felt a quivering sensation in my stomach. But all of this passed when I actually began to speak. I had been over my plans many times with Felipa and *Dona*

Perestrello. As I talked to the king, the words flowed easily. I could tell by his expression that he was interested.

But his advisors kept interrupting me with many objections.

"The distance to Cipangu can be only about fifteen hundred miles," I said. "The ocean is dotted with islands which will make it easy to sail from one to the other."

"That's ridiculous," said one of the advisors. "We all know the Atlantic is a vast ocean with few islands."

"Another thing, too," injected an advisor, "*Senor* Columbus keeps talking of the distances charted by Ptolemy. We all know that Ptolemy was wrong. He made the size of the globe much smaller than it really is."

"And as for Marco Polo," another added his say, "that teller of tall tales could not be trusted in court."

The advisors all laughed at this. But I didn't think it was funny at all. In spite of the objections of his advisors, though, the king did encourage me. He said he would send for me again when he had time to think it over.

That was reasonable enough. I left the meeting that day with the hope that the plan would soon be put into operation.

Bartholomew was not so sure.

"I don't know, Chris," he said, when told about the king. "I really don't trust him. What's to prevent him from stealing your plans and sending someone else?"

"Why would he want to do that?" I asked.

"There are several reasons," Bart explained. "First, you are a foreigner. Secondly, he may not want to grant the titles and the compensation you have asked."

"But there are some things in my favor," I insisted. "The king has been searching for a trade route to India by sending ships down the coast of Africa. So far, he has not been successful. Perhaps he will be willing to try a new and daring plan."

I approached the king several times about my plan. At first he insisted that I needed only one ship. I knew that it would take at least three to carry the men and supplies for such a dangerous journey. Then he and his advisors quibbled over the requests I had made for myself and my family.

In disgust over the delay, I went on a sea voyage down the coast of Africa, hoping that while I was gone the king might change his mind. When I returned, however, I found things at a stalemate, just as they were when I left.

Months passed and nothing happened. The king kept promising me this and that, always keeping my hopes alive, but never doing anything.

I exploded one day while complaining to Bartholomew. "Why doesn't the king do something?" I asked. "I would be very happy with a simple 'yes' or 'no.' "

"I'll tell you why," my brother answered. "It is because the king is thinking that he will discover the route himself by sailing around Africa. Just this past month I heard he had sent out another ship. He is probably waiting for its return."

It was *Dona* Perestrello, my mother-in-law, who told me the bad news about the king that dashed my hopes completely. She had come over from Madeira to visit us because Felipa had been ill.

"The king has been fooling you, Chris," she said when I greeted her.

"What do you mean?" I asked.

Then she told me about a sea captain who had visited Madeira a few days before. He had bragged to her about making a secret voyage for King John a few months earlier.

"What kind of secret voyage?" I inquired.

"Well, this captain," she continued, "said he was under secret orders to sail directly west to reach India."

"What happened?" I exclaimed.

"They sailed directly west. But after a few days, when they had found nothing, the crewmen became very frightened. The captain was forced to return," she said.

"So that's why the king had been putting me off!" I replied bitterly.

"I'm afraid so, my son," she said. "I did not believe the king could be so dishonest."

Meanwhile my lovely Felipa was growing steadily worse. It saddened my heart as I sat by her bed and watched her grow weaker and weaker. Her lovely face, which in earlier days had glowed with beauty, was now pale and lifeless. Her body gradually wasted away.

One day when keeping a lonely vigil beside her, she pulled me down to her and kissed me. I wiped the tears from her eyes and she spoke softly.

"Please take care of Diego," she said.

I nodded, unable to speak to her.

"Christopher," she spoke very softly, "I know that someday you will sail. My prayers will go with you."

That night my lovely Felipa died. She was buried in a little cemetery not far from the church where we first met and where we were married.

Bartholomew was there to comfort me. When we returned home from the funeral, we talked at length of the future.

"I'm leaving Portugal, Bart," I announced. "I have been waiting almost three years for King

John to make up his mind. He has done nothing but trick me."

"I know," said Bart. "We must look somewhere else for help."

"I'm going to try Spain," I said. "I believe that King Ferdinand and Queen Isabella will listen to my plan."

Diego and I boarded a ship in Lisbon and sailed to Palos, in southern Spain. We arrived there on a hot summer day, and with Diego riding on my shoulders, I walked five miles from Palos to the school of La Rabida. I had no money. The expenses of my wife's illness and burial had taken all my savings. I prayed that the good people of La Rabida might take care of Diego for me while I went to present my plan to the king and queen of Spain.

It was not easy for me to ask for charity. But I believed in what I was doing. I also remembered the vows made to my Saviour. I whispered a prayer and rang the bell at the gate.

The man who came to the gate was very kind and ushered us into the courtyard where he provided milk and bread for Diego, who was famished.

Very shortly after our arrival I was interviewed by Father Antonio de Marchena. I asked him if arrangements could be made for the care of my son while I went to Cordova on important business.

"I'll not be able to pay you for awhile," I said, feeling embarrassed over my lack of money.

"That's quite all right," he assured me. "We will be happy for Diego to stay with us. He will not only receive food and shelter, but he will attend classes, too."

"That's wonderful," I said. "I shall forever be

grateful to you, and someday I will repay you for your kindness."

Then I explained to him the purpose of my visit to Spain. He was interested in my project.

"I myself am interested in astronomy and map making," he said. "Perhaps you could stay with us a few days before you begin your journey and tell us more about your plan."

I stayed at La Rabida several days, enjoying their delicious food, and spending long hours talking with the men.

"We believe that the earth is round," one of them explained to me. "We teach that fact here in our school. Your plan to reach India by sailing west will work."

I was much encouraged by these learned men. Before I left, Father Antonio told me of the interest of Martin Pinzon, one of the wealthy shipbuilders in Palos.

"He will support the plan, I am sure," he said.

He also knew the Count of Medina Celi, who was one of the most important men in all of Spain. He owned a large fleet of ships and knew the king and queen personally. Father Antonio wrote a letter of introduction to the count for me.

I was ready now to move on to Cordova. I said good-bye to Diego, knowing he was in good hands and would be well cared for.

The Count of Medina Celi was a wonderful man. He listened carefully as I told him of my plan. He was very excited about it.

"I will underwrite the expedition for you," he said. "I believe in what you are doing."

I almost wept with joy at his words. Never in my long years of waiting had I met anyone, outside my family, who was this excited about the mission.

The count changed his mind, however, when he realized that such a journey might involve the discovery of new territories.

"You must present your plan to the king and queen," he said regretfully. "I will arrange for you to see them."

It was not as easy to see the king and queen as I had thought. Spain was at war with the Moors. I waited in Cordova to be summoned. Long months went by and again I was in despair. I tried to bolster my spirits by thinking of reasons why the Sovereigns of Spain should be interested in my plan.

I knew that the war with the Moors had been very costly. Wouldn't Spain be glad to find a short route to the very rich lands of India? Not only that, but the Pope had given to Portugal the exclusive rights to explore the coasts of Africa. Spanish ships were not even allowed to sail in that direction. The idea that Spanish ships could sail west and beat Portugal to the Indies should be a selling point in my favor.

Finally, after long months of waiting, the word came that I would be received by the king and queen. On the appointed day I dressed in the best suit I had and made my way to the palace. I had to sit for awhile to wait my turn to see the Sovereigns. They were listening to the petitions of others. At last my name was called and I found myself, Christopher Columbus, approaching the throne of Spain.

I bowed before the court. Then standing as tall as I could, I calmly presented my plan to them. I asked for three or four ships to carry men and supplies. I also asked for letters to the sovereign heads of other states that I might visit on my trip.

"And what would you ask for yourself, *Senor* Columbus?" asked the king.

"Your Highness," I replied, "I respectfully ask that I be given the title of Admiral of the Ocean Sea. I respectfully ask that I receive a commission of all the valuable goods collected from the expedition, and that I be made governor over all the lands I may discover."

"That is a large request," replied the king.

"Yes, Your Highness, it is," I replied. "But I am risking my life on a very dangerous mission."

"Is it not true," interrupted Queen Isabella, "that you have approached King John of Portugal with your plan?"

"It is, Your Highness," I replied honestly.

"And he dismissed it as a preposterous suggestion?" she inquired.

"Oh, no, Your Highness," I said. "He did not dismiss it. He sent a secret expedition behind my back!"

Queen Isabella was startled by that bit of news. "Then if what you're telling me is true, why did they not succeed?" she asked.

"Because they lacked a leader who had the courage to stay with it," I replied.

"And you? Do you have that courage?" The queen leaned over in her seat.

"I do, Your Highness," I replied with confidence, looking directly into her eyes.

"Thank you, *Senor* Columbus," the king spoke up. "We will consider your request and call you when we are ready."

So, I was dismissed again, just as I had been dismissed in the Court of King John. But I was not through. I was determined to find a way to fulfill my mission and my vows to the Lord.

The next day I was summoned to the palace again. This time I had a private interview with Queen Isabella. She questioned me at length about my mission.

"One thing I did not mention, Your Highness," I told her, "is the real reason I want to go."

"What is that?" she asked.

"Knowing your most devoted and pious life, I feel that you will be happy to know that I want to evangelize the heathen in lands I shall visit. My one great desire is to carry the news that Christ is the Saviour to the people who have never heard His name."

Then I told the queen of my personal faith in Jesus as my Saviour. I revealed the vows I had made as a child in the little church in Genoa when I promised Jesus I would become a Christ-Bearer for Him, as my name indicated.

The queen was visibly shaken by my testimony. She, too, shared my desires to spread the Gospel of Christ. Unfortunately, the war with the Moors had completely wiped out the treasury. They could not afford even one ship, let alone three.

"But you will go, *Senor* Columbus," she promised. "I will sell my jewels if necessary. You will see."

With that, the queen ordered that I be paid a small monthly wage, for which I was thankful. "When the war is over, and that will be soon," she said, "I will call for you."

But the war dragged on for months, and then into years. I settled down in Cordova and waited for my new day in court.

While I was waiting for news about my trip, I met my second wife. Her name was Beatriz Enriques. She was a cousin of the Harana family who had come from Genoa. In 1488 she bore for me my second son. I named him Ferdinand in honor of the king.

One day Beatriz and I were strolling near our house with little Ferdinand, when I looked up to see my brother Bartholomew.

"Bart!" I said excitedly. "Is it really you?"

"Yes, dear Brother," he replied. "It is I."

We went home to celebrate. Bart wasted no time in telling me the good news.

"I think you should approach King John again, Chris," he said. "Everything is peaceful in Portugal now, and they are not making much progress in their discoveries."

Bart stayed with us a few days and then returned to Lisbon with a letter to King John. In the letter I asked the king for another audience to present once again my plan.

Very shortly I received a reply. The king was indeed interested and wanted to see me. I left immediately by ship from Palos and traveled to Lisbon.

But when I got there, it was the same old story. The king was interested in the plan. But he had just received news that Bartholomew Diaz had rounded the southern tip of Africa and proceeded up the eastern coast. He had discovered the long-awaited sea route to India.

I left Lisbon with all hopes gone that King John would ever sponsor my mission. I went back to Spain with a determination to try once more. If that failed, I would move on to France, or to England, or anywhere. Somebody, somewhere, would wake up someday and send me on the way to do what God wanted me to do!

admiral of
the ocean sea

The war with the Moors dragged on. Year after year the battles raged. It became obvious that Spain was fighting for her life.

Meanwhile, I waited in Cordova, Spain, with Beatriz and Ferdinand. Occasionally I visited Diego at La Rabida in Italy. The faithful men there would join with me in prayer for my mission.

I grew impatient, longing for the sea, anxious to sail away from that troubled land. Again I wrote to Bartholomew. He answered me with a long letter stating that he was going to England and France to get support for my mission. He hoped to convince King Henry of England or King Charles of France that our mission was a worthy project.

Then suddenly the war came to an end. On January 2, 1492 the royal procession entered the city of Granada, the last stronghold of the Moslem Moors. Victory at last! I believed now that the war was over the king and queen would send me on my great enterprise.

The next few days were filled with excitement. I waited patiently to see the king and queen.

Finally, a messenger came with a summons for me to appear. The queen enclosed a personal note and a modest sum of money.

I rushed out to purchase a new suit of clothes because I wanted to look my best. I also purchased a mule. The difficult task of keeping up with the king and queen as they moved about all over the country had become too much for me!

On the following day I presented myself before the king and queen. I was confident they were ready for me to begin my great mission.

But my hopes were soon dashed. They told me the whole idea was off! Queen Isabella broke the sad news.

"As you know, *Senor* Columbus," she said, "we have had a group of scholars studying your proposal for some time."

"Yes, Your Highness," I replied. "I was aware of that." A panel of experts had been appointed by the crown to study my proposal. They had been working on it for almost seven years!

"We have decided on the basis of their strong recommendation," continued the queen, "that your plan is not feasible for us at the moment. Therefore we are turning down your request for men and ships."

The words of the queen hit me like a storm on the sea. I will never know how I managed to leave that palace without saying what I felt in my heart. I was angry, frustrated, and disappointed beyond words.

When I did leave, I went home to say good-bye to Beatriz and Ferdinand. Then I mounted my mule for the long ride to La Rabida. I planned to get Diego and leave him with some friends and then go immediately to France.

I had been insulted, degraded, and kicked around long enough by the royalty of Spain. For almost seven years they had led me to believe they would finance my mission, and now, this final insult.

"Well, I will show them!" I muttered to myself as I guided my mule down the dusty road toward Palos. "I've had enough of their Spanish hospitality. Now I will go to France. Perhaps Bartholomew will have some good news for me there."

I had traveled about ten miles when I heard a horseman approaching from the rear. I did not stop, but kept doggedly on. Then I heard a voice as the horseman got nearer.

"*Senor* Columbus!" he called. "Wait, I have a message from the queen!"

I turned my mule around to face the messenger. "A message from the queen?" I asked. "What does she want?"

"She asks that you turn around and come to the castle immediately," the man said. Then with a twinkle in his eye he said, "I think it is good news, sir!"

Reluctantly at first, I made my way back to Cordova. When I arrived at the castle, I found that my good friend Luis de Santangel had persuaded the king and queen to reconsider. He was the keeper of the royal purse and naturally, his word carried a bit of weight with King Ferdinand and Queen Isabella.

Later I learned how he had done it. His argument had been so simple, yet so true. He said to them, "You ought to give this man a chance. After all, the cost of outfitting the mission is so little, and the prospect of what he may discover is so great." He had challenged the monarchs to think, "What have we got to lose?" When they began to think in those terms, they decided to give me what I needed for the enterprise of the Indies!

It took us three months to negotiate the terms of our agreement. But when we had finished I was satisfied. I had received every consideration requested and more.

In a long, public document the king and queen outlined the terms of the agreement. First, I was given the title of Admiral in and over all the islands and mainlands which I might discover. Secondly, I was appointed Viceroy and Governor-General over all the lands I might discover. Then I was given a tenth of all the profits which might result from the discoveries. Furthermore, all these rights and privileges were to be passed on to my heirs and successors forever.

I wrote Bartholomew, who had become a mapmaker in the Court of King Charles of France, to tell him the good news.

"Dear Bart," I wrote to him. "I wanted you to

sail with me. But there will not be time. In fact, you will not even receive this letter before I am gone. We sail in two weeks!"

I should have known better. There was no way we could secure three ships and outfit them for a voyage such as this in two weeks. But the date had been set and I hastened to Palos to begin work immediately.

The townspeople of Palos were not in a receptive mood. Sometime in the distant past the town had violated some of the provisions of the Sovereigns of Spain. As a result, a decree had been signed which ordered them to furnish two ships to the state as payment of their obligation. Now the queen was pressing them for payment. They were supposed to furnish two of the ships needed for the expedition.

Since they were struggling themselves to meet the bare necessities of life, they resented the queen's order, which came at a very bad time.

If it had not been for my long friendship with Martin Alonso Pinzon and his brothers Francisco and Vincente, I would have had a bad time in Palos. But they rallied to my cause, and because they were the most respected citizens in the town, things became easier.

The ships were secured. First, the townspeople of Palos supplied me with two ships of the type called caravels. They were named the *Pinta* and the *Nina*. Since both of these were small caravels, I looked around for a larger ship to serve as the flagship for the fleet. I found a ship suitable for the purpose, called *La Gallega* (the Woman of Galicia). I immediately changed the name of the ship to *Santa Maria* (Holy Mary) in honor of the mother of Jesus. After all, it would be a ship destined to carry the good news of our Saviour to

foreign shores. It deserved a name which fitted its noble purpose!

When the ships had been secured, the work of outfitting them and supplying a crew had to begin. Martin Pinzon came to my aid.

"I want to sail with you, *Don* Columbus," he said one day. "And I will help you sign up a crew for the three ships."

Then he began talking to the local men. He would say to them, "Look, life is miserable for you here in Palos. Come with us and you can make a fortune in a few weeks. We are going to a land where the houses are domed with gold." Then if that were not enough, he would say, "Man, this is the chance of a lifetime. You will never have another opportunity like this." With that kind of persuasive argument he was able to sign up the ninety men we needed.

But the work on the ships went very slowly. The two weeks passed and days slipped into months as we struggled to make the necessary repairs and to stock the provisions needed for a long voyage.

We needed much food. I stood at the docks day after day and watched the men as they loaded hoops of cheese, giant tubs of salt meat and fish, casks of wine and water, and quantities of wheat which would be baked into biscuits for the crew.

We also loaded Hawks' bells and brightly colored red caps which were used by the Portuguese for trading with the natives in Africa. Through the hot summer months we labored, outfitting and supplying the ships with everything we needed to sail the ocean seas.

I personally supervised the alterations on the flagship *Santa Maria*. We added a topsail to the main mast, which would make her sail faster in the blue waters of the Atlantic. We also outfitted a cabin on the forecastle which would make the journey more pleasant and comfortable for me.

During the hot days of July when work on the ships was progressing, it became obvious that we would soon be able to sail.

"Pass the word along to the men," I said to Martin Pinzon one day. "We will sail at dawn on Friday, August 3."

The word soon flashed around the town of Palos. There was excitement in the air! At last we would be on our way! Townspeople stopped each other to talk about the voyage. Mothers and wives of the crewmen became anxious. Many of them feared they would never see their men again. They worried about sea monsters and wondered if the world really was round.

Beatriz, Ferdinand, and Diego came down to Palos to spend a few days with me before we sailed. I was happy to know that Diego was now being cared for by Beatriz. My family was together.

"Father," Diego said excitedly as they arrived. "I have some news for you!"

"What is it, my son?" I asked, before I even had time to greet Beatriz.

"I have been appointed to serve Prince Juan as a page!"

I could tell my son was thrilled at his appointment which I had arranged through correspondence with Queen Isabella. She had been impressed with Diego's manners and knowledge which he had acquired at La Rabida. She felt he would be a good influence on the child, Prince Juan. The teachers at La Rabida had done their work well.

"I am sorry Bartholomew is not here to sail with me," I said later to Beatriz. "Please tell him that I want him with me on the next voyage."

"He will understand, I am sure," Beatriz assured me.

"Meanwhile, I ask that you might keep my family together," I said to Beatriz.

"I will, Christopher," she promised. "We will wait together for your return."

Friday, August 3, 1492 was a day I shall always remember. I was up early, hours before dawn, to go with the men who would sail with me to the Church of St. George in Palos. There we listened to the special prayers for the voyage. In the darkness of those early morning hours I knelt before God and renewed my vows to take the message of the Saviour to foreign lands. I prayed that God might go with us as we sailed through the uncharted seas before us.

All the men prayed that morning. I am sure they were thinking of the dangers that lay ahead and wondering if they would ever kneel in that church again. God's blessing was invoked upon us. We departed from the church immediately to the ships that would take us away.

The townspeople gathered to say their farewells. Beatriz and my two sons were there for a few brief moments. While talking with them, I heard a murmur running through the crowd.

"Fall back!" The command rumbled through the crowd. "King Ferdinand and Queen Isabella are here!"

We all fell on our knees before the royal entourage. King Ferdinand and Queen Isabella approached, walking slowly with a group of their protectors.

It was the queen who spoke to me. "*Don* Columbus, we have come to bid you farewell and to say our prayers are with you as you go."

I could not speak to the queen. My heart was filled with joy, my eyes misty with tears. I tried to mumble some words of thanksgiving to both of them for their kindnesses. Then I retreated to the safety of the ship, mounted my position of command, and proudly gave the order that set our fleet in motion.

The order was a simple one.

"Weigh the anchors and proceed in the name of Jesus," I commanded the ship's pilot, Peralonso Nino. He in turn broadcast the command. The anchors were weighed and the sails unfurled. The red cross of Christ painted on each of the sails glistened in the dawning rays of the sun. Yes, Christ had died on the cross for me and the people we would meet in the new lands ahead!

Beatriz, Ferdinand, and Diego stood on the docks and waved as the ships glided out of the harbor and into the Saltes River which would take us to the sea. Beatriz wiped her eyes with the handkerchief she was holding and cried.

In just a few minutes we were sailing down the river, past the school of La Rabida where I had gone so many years before with little Diego. I remembered that hot summer day when the men had opened the gate to their school and had encouraged me to go on with my dreams.

Now they were chanting the early morning prayers. Their voices lifted up over the Saltes River as we passed, and I heard the familiar words of the hymn:

> Glory be to God the Father,
> And to His only Son,
> With the Spirit, the Paraclete
> Both now and forever!

I bowed my head and whispered my vow to God. "Now and forever!" I said as I committed the voyage to Jesus. My mind went back to that day, many years before, when I had knelt in the little church in Genoa with my mother and promised the Lord to become a Christ-Bearer for Him.

It had been ten long years since I first presented my plan to King John of Portugal. Those had been years of frustration, disappointment, and sadness. But now, my patience was rewarded. I looked up in time to see that we were crossing the bar of the Saltes River, some three miles downstream from Palos. The ships glided smoothly into the calm, still waters of the sea, their sails gleaming in the rising sun.

There was much work to be done. I lifted my eyes to look upon the waters and set the course that would take us onward. I was Christopher Columbus, Admiral of the Ocean Sea! Praise God! The Christ-Bearer was on his way at last!

Landfall!

Sailing on that first day out from Palos was easy. Land was in sight all day. That night however, the course of the ships was set for the Canary Islands, south by west. We used a pitch-pine torch to signal the other two ships in the fleet, and shortly after sunset we were on our way.

Some of the men had objected to the use of the Canary Islands as a launching point. In a conference held several days before we sailed they had voiced their opinions.

"But why don't we sail from the Azores?" one of the men had asked. "They are much further west than the Canaries."

I knew, and Martin Pinzon knew, that our reason for choosing the Canaries was because of the wind currents. Anyone who had ever sailed the Portuguese ships down the African coast knew that the prevailing westerly winds were best at the Canaries.

I kept my peace however, and insisted that we sail from the Canaries. The matter was settled that night as our fleet sailed in harmony toward the Canary Islands.

The ocean between Spain and the Canary Islands is a rough bit of sea. The sailors called it the Sea of the Mares. For almost a century Spanish traders had carried on a lively trade in horses with the Canary Islands. Because so many horses had died on the treacherous trip to the Canaries, sailors had come to believe the trip was jinxed with bad luck.

We were only three days out from Palos when we discovered just how rough it really was. Giant waves rolled under and over the three ships constantly, creating a motion that caused even the hardened sailors to wonder if the sea would ever be calm again. They were restless waves, moving without letup, and seemingly without much wind. Our ships rolled and pitched and I found it difficult to keep them on course. Several times we came dangerously close to colliding with another ship in the fleet, but managed to shift the sails at the last moment to prevent a smashup.

The big rudder on the *Pinta* jumped its gudgeons, and the little ship sent out a distress signal. We pulled alongside, and using the ship's boat, I went over to the *Pinta* to have a look.

Martin Pinzon was the captain of the *Pinta*. He was disturbed by the broken rudder.

"I think it was done deliberately," he confided with me as we sat in the captain's cabin.

"What do you mean?" I asked my friend.

"Cristobal Quintero, the owner of this ship, has done nothing but complain since we left," explained Martin. "He was unhappy because the queen commandeered his ship for this voyage."

"And you think Quintero wrecked his own ship?" I asked in disbelief.

"I do," replied Martin.

"But he is sailing with us," I reminded Martin. "Surely, he would not endanger his own life in these rough seas."

"He knows we are sailing to the Canaries," insisted Martin. "He feels that if the ship is damaged we will not sail beyond there."

"But I assure you, my friend, we will fix the rudder in the Canaries and we will sail on."

"May it be so," muttered Martin. I could tell by the tone of his voice that he still held Quintero responsible for our troubles.

Fortunately, we were able to repair the rudder so that we could continue our trip to the Canary Islands. We made it there in six days, which was very good sailing time in anybody's record, and that with a bad rudder on one ship!

We left the *Pinta* at Las Palmas on the Grand Canary Island while we sailed on to Gromera, the capital. There I hoped to see *Dona* Beatriz Bobadilla, the gracious ruler of the islands.

I had heard about this attractive young widow who ruled the islands for the crown. The gossip around the court of Spain was that Queen Isabella had been jealous of *Dona* Beatriz, a beautiful young lady who had all the nobles of Spain flocking after her. When Hernan Perazo, the ruler of the Canary Islands, had been accused of murder, he was pardoned by the queen in return for marrying Beatriz and taking her back to the Canaries. This, according to the court gossip, solved the problem for the queen by removing Beatriz from Spain. Hernan Perazo was killed shortly after their marriage. *Dona* Beatriz had been appointed ruler in his place.

It was not the widow's beauty, nor the gossip I had heard about her, that made me want to see her. I wanted to make a deal, if possible, for another caravel to replace the *Pinta*, which had

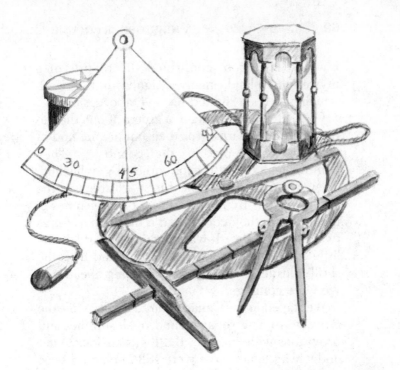

developed a bad leak in addition to the rudder problems.

Dona Beatriz told me stories of men in the islands who swore under oath that they had sailed west and seen another island which they called *San Borondon*.

"I have heard of the mysterious island," I told *Dona* Beatriz. "I plan to visit it on the way to the Indies."

I had not told anyone this, but I was counting on that island as a stopping place to help us get across the vast expanse of the Atlantic. Since it had been sighted supposedly by men who had never reached it, I had its approximate position already marked on my charts.

In addition to my visit with *Dona* Beatriz, I also visited and talked with some of the natives of the island. They too, confirmed the reports of a mysterious island, many leagues to the west, which had been sighted on several occasions.

One interesting thing I learned about the natives of the Canaries was their unique method of communication out in the country. They communicated with each other by whistling. They were probably the finest whistlers in the whole world. By means of two or three notes in their whistle they could send a message as far as two or three miles. It was amazing to stand on the little road out from San Sebastian and hear the shrill whistles of the natives signaling ahead that we were coming.

We stayed in the Canaries three weeks while the *Pinta* was being repaired and fresh supplies and provisions were loaded. But I was anxious to get under way again. We were still in charted seas, and I wanted to sail in uncharted waters.

In the early hours of September 6 we went to church as we had done at Palos before we sailed. Then, saying good-bye to *Dona* Beatriz, we went aboard ship, and weighing the anchors, sailed away from Gromera.

The winds were light and variable, however, and for two days we were becalmed, still in sight of land. On the second day, with all of us growing restless and anxious to be moving, we said special prayers during our evening worship time. The following morning the Lord answered our prayers. The winds picked up. We unfurled the sails, and the land behind us disappeared in the distance.

We sailed due west. In the evenings the bows of our ships glided into the rays of the sun directly ahead. In the mornings the sun rose behind us, over the great continent of Africa, throwing its shimmering rays on the sea.

I would stand on the deck and feel the first
warm rays of the morning sun on my face as the
crewmen stirred in the early hours of the day. The
brisk morning air, mixed with the soft, salty spray
of the sea always waked me to the promise of a
new day that could be lived for my Lord.

The mornings were my favorite time at sea.
After one of those beautiful, breathtaking
mornings I described the beauty of it in the journal
for that day.

> *It is like April in Andalusia. Nothing is*
> *missing except the nightingales. How great a*
> *pleasure is the taste of the mornings!*

On the first night of our journey out of Palos I
had begun keeping a journal with the words: "In
the Name of Our Lord Jesus Christ . . . ." I
intended it to be an account of my mission as a
Christ-Bearer for the Lord. At night I recorded all
that we had seen and done the day before, and in
the mornings all that had transpired during the
night.

I found a young lad among our crew who
reminded me of myself when I was his age. His
name was Pedro. One day when I was walking on
deck, I spotted Pedro and called him.

"What's your name, lad?" I asked, although I
already knew.

"Pedro de Salcedo, sir," he replied. "I am at
your service, sir."

His courteous manners and interest in sailing
had already commanded my attention.

"Would you like to serve me in my cabin?" I
asked Pedro.

"I certainly would, sir," he replied.

"Then come with me," I said, "and you will be
my cabin boy."

From that day on, Pedro served me faithfully. He brought me breakfast in the mornings and tended to all my personal needs. He also kept the cabin spotlessly clean.

I taught Pedro how to read the compass and how to use the quadrant.

"The quadrant is a simple instrument," I explained to Pedro. "But it is very important. It helps you determine your position by the use of the stars." Then I demonstrated how to move the plumb line to position it with Polaris so that our true position might be noted.

I shared with Pedro the Scriptures I had noted in my journal about the stars: "When I consider thy heavens, the work of thy fingers, the moon and the stars, which thou hast ordained; What is man, that thou art mindful of him? and the son of man, that thou visitest him? For thou has made him a little lower than the angels, and hast crowned him with glory and honour" (Psalm 8:3-5).

Pedro told me that he was a Christian and that he too shared my faith in Jesus as a redeeming Lord. We rejoiced together in the knowledge that our Lord was so real to both of us.

"But how can you tell, sir, how far you have sailed and in what direction to sail?" Pedro asked, bringing us back to the instructions.

"I use a system which is called 'dead reckoning,'" I explained carefully. "By estimating the distance we have traveled, and determining the previously set course, I can make adjustments in our directions that will be accurate most of the time."

"There are some on board that think you can smell land, sir," Pedro said.

"What do you mean?" I asked.

"They believe you are a very good sailor, and that you have some kind of special sense that directs you in the sea," replied my little friend.

I was pleased to know that the crewmen had respect for the special abilities my Saviour had given me to navigate the seas.

All went well for those first few days in the open seas. The days were greeted by the young man who chanted the morning hymn:

> *Blessed be the light of day.*
> *And the Holy Cross, we say;*
> *And the Lord of Veritie*
> *And the Holy Trinity.*

This was followed by the prayer: "God give us good days, good voyage, good passage to the ship, sir captain and master and good company, so let there be, let there be a good voyage."

One morning shortly after the prayers had been said, Pedro came into my cabin with a troubled look on his face.

"What's troubling you, my son?" I asked as I gently plucked at his chin.

"Master, there are men on board who say that we will never see land again," he cried.

"Oh," I said cheerfully, "we will see land again. Don't you worry." Then I asked him, "Just what are they saying, lad?"

"They say that we will never find the winds that will blow us back to Spain," the boy replied. "Then one man said there were giant fish in the ocean that would swallow the ships. Still another said we would reach the end of the sea and drop off into a terrible space!"

"You don't really believe those old seamen tales, do you?" I placed my arm around him. "Why, they've been saying things like that for centuries. But no one has ever seen a fish big enough to swallow a ship, or a place where the sea drops off into nothing."

"That may be so, sir," Pedro was comforted some. "But what about the winds. We have had nothing but westerly winds blowing us away from land. Suppose we never find any winds that will blow us back."

"Well, my boy," I said. "Don't you worry about that. When the time comes for us to go home, we will find the winds to carry us there."

"But what shall I tell the men, Master?" asked Pedro. "They are growing restless and afraid because we have traveled so far."

I paused for a moment to think my answer through clearly. "Tell them," I said, "that when the time comes the Master will find the winds to take us home. But right now, we must look for land ahead."

I knew the men were growing restless. I could tell as I walked about on the ship. It was not so much what they said, as how they said it. The inflections and tones of their voices told me much about how they felt.

Then one day I overheard a crewman as he muttered to several others, "What does *Don* Columbus think we are?"

Then another piped up. "How far does he think he can push us? I think the time has come for us to turn around."

Several of the men nodded their heads in agreement. I wondered if there would be open mutiny on the ship.

I called a general meeting to help calm the situation. I told the men that we should be near land.

"Haven't we seen signs of land?" I asked. It had been reported to me that pieces of carved wood had been found, and birds had been spotted — sure signs land was near. But I was in no mood to placate them so I spoke frankly. "There is no point in your asking me to turn back. I am going to the Indies and I shall sail on until, with God's help, I find them."

But the grumbling continued. Finally, it got so bad on the other ships that Martin Pinzon and his brother Vincente, captain of the *Nina*, called for a council meeting. We met aboard the *Santa Maria*.

Martin Pinzon was furious. He spoke of the troublemakers.

"Hang them!" he said to me. "If you don't, I and my brother will."

I did not encourage the Pinzons in this. I wanted to keep peace aboard the ships. However, I let it be known that day that we would not tolerate mutiny in any fashion.

Just as we had matters under control, we sailed into a sea of weeds. I had heard about the areas called a sargasso sea from old-time sailors. This was the first time I'd seen one of these places in the ocean. It was a little frightening at first. The sea was completely covered for many miles with the seaweed known as sargasso. Some of the sailors were frightened and felt that the ships would become entangled in the weeds and we would all perish.

On October 7, after we had been at sea for a whole month and the men on the ships were very jittery, we had a false landfall call. The *Nina* fired her gun and hoisted a flag to indicate that she had sighted land. There was much excitement as we all peered ahead to see what looked like land in the distance. But it turned out to be only an accumulation of clouds on the distant horizon, shaped like mountains rising up from the sea.

But we had observed flocks of birds all day flying toward the south. As an experienced sailor I knew that birds could only fly certain distances from land. They have to light sometimes to rest

from their flights. I finally agreed with Martin
Pinzon that we should alter our course to west by
south, in the direction the birds were flying.

On the tenth day of October another council
was called. It was evident that the men would not
go on much further without sighting land. It
seemed that my dreams of finding the Indies by
sailing west were about to fail, in spite of the fact
that we had sailed further from land than anyone
else before us.

Reluctantly I agreed that if we did not find land
after pressing on for three more days, we would
turn back and head for Spain. But I was confident
we could find land.

"I believe we are close to land," I told the Pinzon
brothers. "Pass the word that I will give a silk
doublet to the first man who sights it, in addition to
the queen's reward."

On Thursday, October 11, the trade winds were
blowing swiftly. We picked up several signs of
land ahead. The *Nina* picked up a little flower
from the sea. The *Pinta* found a little stick which
seemed to be fastened to a piece of iron. The men
were all encouraged so that everyone breathed
more freely and grew cheerful.

The prayers were sung that night with a
fervency I had not heard in weeks. Everyone was
in a mood of gaiety, expecting that we would find
land at any moment. After the evening prayers,
when things had quieted down a bit, I retired to
my cabin with Pedro to continue praying.

About ten o'clock I was looking out ahead when
I thought I saw a light flickering in the distance. I
remembered that night many years ago when
flickering lights near Lisbon had kept me alive
with hope as I swam in the sea. Now another
mysterious light kept my hopes alive.

"Pedro," I called. "Do you see a light ahead?"

Pedro climbed on the table to peer ahead in the darkness. "Yes, Master," he said excitedly, "I believe I do!"

I sent Pedro immediately to fetch Peralonso Nino, the ship's pilot. When he arrived, I asked if he could see the light. He, too, thought he saw it, although he was not as sure as I. The light seemed to be moving about as I watched it.

Finally, someone on the *Nina*, running ahead of us, saw the light and flashed a signal. Then we signaled in return that we had already spotted it.

At two o'clock on the morning of October 12 there was a great turmoil aboard the *Pinta*. Rodrigo de Triana, a sailor aboard the *Pinta* cried out, "Land in sight!" Guns were fired, flags were hoisted, and general bedlam broke loose on all three ships.

There was no doubt about it, this time. Land was clearly visible ahead in the moonlight. I immediately fell on my knees and thanked God for His blessings.

"When will we land, Master?" Pedro asked. He was so excited he could not be still.

"Tomorrow, Pedro. Tomorrow we shall go ashore and claim the land for the king and queen and for our Lord!"

islands in the sea

Through the night we waited off shore. I had ordered the ships to reduce their sails lest we be driven onto the rocks and dashed to pieces. None of us slept any that night; the excitement was too great.

I thought of Bartholomew as I waited through the long morning hours. If only he could be here to share these moments of triumph with me. After thirty-three days of sailing the uncharted seas we had reached land at last!

Suddenly the day dawned. We could see clearly white cliffs and tall palm trees on the land. Shortly after daybreak we could see figures running down to the shore.

"I can't believe what I am seeing," cried Peralonso Nino, the pilot. "They are all as naked as the day they were born!"

I looked at the natives who had already gathered near the shore, waiting for our arrival. Peralonso was right! None of them had on any clothes.

I left the deck and went to my cabin where Pedro was perched on the table, watching the natives on the land.

"Where are the cities with the houses made of gold, Master?" Pedro asked.

"We are probably a long way from the cities, Pedro. But we must go ashore and find out more about this land we have found," I said.

While Pedro was laying out my best clothes and preparing my breakfast, I went out on the deck again just as Martin Pinzon and his brother, Vincente, came scrambling over the rails. They told me of the excitement on their ships.

"Our men are anxious to go ashore," reported Vincente.

"We must go first," I declared, "to claim the land for Our Majesties."

"Then we will follow the plan we agreed upon before sailing?" asked Martin.

"Absolutely," I said. "You men go back to your ships and put on your best clothes. We will pick you up in one hour." With that I dismissed them and returned to my cabin.

Pedro had breakfast ready. I ate hurriedly, then hastened to put on my best clothes. I wore for the occasion, a green silk doublet and a bright red cape — the same outfit I had worn when I stood before the Sovereigns of Spain to receive my commission.

When I was ready, Peralonso lowered the ship's boat. We chose a few men from the *Santa Maria* to go with us. Rowing over to the *Pinta* we picked up Martin Pinzon, then rowed over to the *Nina* to pick up Vincente.

I carried in my hand the royal standard. Martin and Vincente each carried the banner of the expedition, a green cross with the initials of King

Ferdinand on one and the initials of Queen Isabella on the other.

Slowly, the little boat approached the shore. The natives who had gathered to watch the proceedings, backed up a bit, and watched us intently.

I was the first to step onto the land. We walked ashore for a few yards and then fell on our knees, claiming the land for King Ferdinand and Queen Isabella, and for our Lord. The banners were set in the sandy beaches while we uttered prayers of thanksgiving to God.

Rodrigo de Escobedo, the official secretary of our expedition, witnessed the solemn transfer of the land to the Sovereigns of Spain.

Other boats were arriving, carrying more of the men in our fleet. To my complete surprise they came and bowed down before me. Tears were streaming down their faces.

"Forgiveness, forgiveness!" they begged.

One of the men stood before the group. I recognized him as one of the leaders of those who had wanted to turn back.

"We beg your forgiveness, Your Majesty," he exclaimed. "We recognize you as Admiral and Viceroy of all that is before us!"

With the exultant joy of one who has fulfilled a dream, and with the peace of my Lord in my soul, I forgave them gladly.

Meanwhile, the natives which I called "Indians" watched us with fascination. We approached them cautiously at first, but observed that they had no weapons at all. Soon they were bringing us gifts of fruit.

Since they showed so much friendship for us, and because they were clearly a people who would better become members of the Christian faith by love than by force, I gave to some of them colored caps and to others glass beads for their necks, as well as many other things of little value. They were delighted with these things and were so friendly to us that it was quite marvelous. Later on they came out swimming to the ships' boats, and brought us parrots, balls of cotton thread, darts, and many other things.

They were well-built people, handsome, with coarse short hair which they wore shaggy over their eyebrows. Some of them had painted their bodies all over with bright colors; others painted their faces only.

I stood with Martin Pinzon on the forecastle of the *Santa Maria* later that day and watched the excitement of our men as the Indians swam out to the ships.

"These people ought to make good and skillful helpers," I said to Martin. "They imitate our speech very quickly."

"Yes, I have noticed that," said Martin.

"I noticed, too," I continued, "that they do not seem to have any religion of their own. I am sure they will easily become Christians!"

"Sir, did you notice the rings of gold dangling from their noses?" Martin asked me.

"Yes," I replied. "I did. Do you think that has something to do with their religion?"

"I don't know about religion, sir," replied Martin. "I'll leave that up to you. I'm interested in the gold. And so, I might add, are Their Highnesses, Ferdinand and Isabella."

I detected in Martin's voice a hint of arrogance and my senses told me that there would be trouble ahead with this man. I only hoped his greed for gold would not replace my desire to see the Christian religion brought to these lands we had discovered together.

The next day, Saturday October 13, we went ashore to explore the land (Watkin's Island, Bahamas) more completely. We learned that the land was an island, and I immediately christened it *San Salvador* (Saint Saviour) in honor of our Lord Jesus.

We managed to communicate some with the Indians by using sign language. By touching the gold rings and pointing, we learned that the gold came from another land to the south. The Indian word for that land was *Cubanacan* (Cuba). That word sounded familiar to me. Could this be the fabulous land of the Kubla Khan I had read about in *The Travels of Marco Polo*? It certainly sounded like it, and I determined that we must sail on and find that land.

We decided to sail the next day. I persuaded several of the Indians to go with us to act as guides. They soon understood us, either by speech or by signs. They were very useful. They were quite convinced that I was from heaven and wherever we went, they announced this fact. Dashing from house to house in the villages, they cried out, "Come and see the people from heaven!"

We sailed west from San Salvador and on the following day, found a second island, which I named *Santa Maria de la Concepcion* (Rum Cay). It was here that we first observed the Indians in their native canoes. The canoes were hewn from a single log and moved swiftly. Some of our men discovered this when they tried to catch one with their clumsy little ship's boat. Some of the canoes were quite large. We saw one with as many as seventy or eighty men aboard, each paddling expertly!

The next island we found I named *Fernandina* (Long Island) in honor of our king. The Indians here told us that there were hundreds of islands further south and that gold abounded. We were convinced that we were on the way to the fabulous lands of the East.

On the northern side of that island we anchored for awhile and the men went ashore to visit an Indian village for the first time. They carried the usual trinkets for trading and actually entered the houses of the friendly natives. When they returned to the ships, they were full of exciting stories, mostly about the beds the Indians slept in.

One of the sailors on the *Santa Maria*, Luis, reported to me.

"The beds they sleep in are like nets of cotton," he said excitedly.

"What do they call them?" I asked, curious about this thing which had fascinated my men.

"They call them *hamacas*," reported Luis, "and they can be strung from one tree to another, or almost anywhere. I'll bet they could even be set up on a ship!"

Luis was talking about the hammock, a type of bed that later became standard equipment on Spanish ships. We saw them first on Fernandina.

We also observed for the first time the strange barkless dogs which the Indians kept as pets, and sometimes ate for food.

Soon we discovered another island which I named *Isabella* (Saomete) in honor of our beloved queen. We landed here for awhile and explored the rich fertile land. It was here, near a lagoon in the center of the island, where Spanish sailors drew their swords and butchered a hideous reptile with a great mouth. The Indians called it a *iguana* (horned lizard). We were to see many of them in the new lands we had found.

It was raining most of the time we were in these islands, although it was very warm. Since the natives did not wear clothing, we assumed that the weather was like this all the time.

On Sunday, October 28 we sailed for the land many of the Indians had told us about. Some called it *Cubanacan* (Cuba), others called it *Colba*. I was sure they were all talking about the fabulous land of the Kubla Khan. There would be much gold there, I was sure; enough to make the treasury of our Sovereigns overflow.

We found a large island, bigger than England and Scotland put together, which our native guides identified as Colba. The mountains stretched into the sky and reminded me of the mountain ranges of Sicily which I had seen when I was a boy.

We sailed into the mouth of a large river and anchored. The men went out to search for the cities. All we found, however, was a deserted Indian village, inhabited by a few strange barkless dogs. Later our men did find the Indians, settled in a remote village of huts. They reported to me, however, that this was certainly not China, and they had been unable to find the great Khan.

I determined to sail eastward from this point because I believed the mainland was in that direction. In a conference aboard the *Santa Maria* I discussed the situation with my captains.

"Where do you think we should go next?" asked Martin Pinzon.

"We must be near India," I insisted. "The natives here who are dark-skinned and who wear no clothes remind me of the descriptions I have read of India."

"Yes, that is true," Martin agreed. "But we must find the gold!"

"We will find plenty of gold, Martin," I assured him. "The Indians tell us that the lands beyond are filled with it."

"So where do we go next?" he asked again.

"We sail eastward — in the direction the Indians gave us."

When we left the island of Colba, Martin Pinzon deserted us. The *Pinta*, which was a swifter vessel than the *Santa Maria*, simply sailed off and left us. No doubt the greed for gold caused the captain to sail on without us. I am thankful to God that Vincente, his brother who captained the *Nina*, did not desert us, too.

On December 12, we took possession of another island for King Ferdinand and Queen Isabella. The Indians called the island *Haiti*, but because it reminded me so much of Spain itself, I called it *Hispaniola* (Little Spain).

The natives of Hispaniola were friendly, and things seemed to be getting better and better. They, too, told us of other lands where gold flowed in the streams of the river. The men were much encouraged by these reports.

Here I became acquainted with my first native *cacique* (ruler) of the Indians. His name was Guacanagari. He gave me a splendid gift, a belt made of cotton, but having in its center the face of a god made out of gold. So, the Indians did have gods of some kind. I made a mental note of this and determined that on my next voyage we would bring with us missionaries who could tell the Indians of our God.

Guacanagari told us that in the interior of the island there was a gold mine. I also noted this fact and decided we would come back later and explore the gold mine. But we had to press on and find the land of India soon. Especially now, I knew Martin Pinzon was already out ahead of us.

A few days before Christmas we were drifting off the coast of Hispaniola when we were struck by a heavy storm. The winds came unexpectedly and pounded us with terrific force. The ship groaned and creaked under the strain. Giant waves pushed across the deck of the *Santa Maria* as sailors hustled to draw in the thundering sails. There was nothing we could do but wait it out. I remembered other storms I had encountered and searched for a rocky cove for protection. We soon found one and slipped our ships inside to wait out the storm.

On Christmas Eve I decided to go to bed early. The storm had abated somewhat. I believed that by morning it would be over. I left Juan de la Costa in charge of the evening watch and had my evening devotions in the cabin with Pedro.

"Tomorrow is Christmas Day, Master," Pedro reminded me after we had said our prayers.

"Yes, Pedro, it is true," I replied. "It will be the first Christmas ever to be celebrated by Christians in this pagan land."

I went to sleep very quickly, because I had not had much rest lately. I awoke during the night due to a gentle bump of the ship.

"We've hit something!" was my first thought as I leaped out of bed. Then I heard the men running and shouting and realized the ship had struck a reef.

I ordered the ship's boat lowered to take an anchor out astern. I hoped that this would kedge the ship off the reef. But it was too late.

Some of the men had left to signal the *Nina* that we were in trouble. By the time the *Nina* arrived, great seams were being ripped in the hull. Sadly, I gave the order to abondon the ship.

Vincente Pinzon spent the night hauling the crew from the wrecked ship to the *Nina*. I was the last one to leave, but finally climbed aboard the overcrowded little ship in the waning hours of the night, drenched to the bone.

"Vincente," I said, when I could finally speak, "you have acted very bravely tonight. You have saved the lives of our men. I am very proud of you."

"It was nothing, nothing at all," Vincente replied, but I could tell he was pleased with my words of praise.

"Well, there goes our Christmas," complained Pedro.

"Be thankful that you are alive, my boy," I heard someone tell Pedro. "We all could have been killed."

"Yes," replied Pedro. "You are right, of course. I should be thankful we are alive."

I wondered about tomorrow as I stood there on the deck of the *Nina*. What would we do now with only one ship and few provisions? Martin Pinzon and the *Pinta* were nowhere in sight. For the first time on our voyage I was homesick. I longed to see Beatriz, and Ferdinand and Diego and Bartholomew. I even thought how I would like to ride my mule down the dusty roads of Spain again.

Perhaps I would someday. But now I had to think of how we might get home. There was only one way. I went to the ship's cabin, fell on my knees, and prayed that my Saviour would show me the way.

homeward
Bound!

Christmas Day, which we had hoped to
celebrate by feasting with the friendly Indians,
was spent in salvaging the provisions and supplies
from the wrecked *Santa Maria*. All hands worked
throughout the day bringing the supplies from the
ship.

Guacanagari, the friendly Indian chief, brought
men with him and joined in the salvaging
operations. The Indians worked right along with
our men and helped remove everything from the
ship. Not a single item was lost or taken by the
Indians, not even a needle!

In the afternoon of that Christmas Day, I was
still awaiting some word from God about what to
do. Guacanagari was invited aboard the *Nina* for
a simple meal with Vincente Pinzon and myself.
He told us while we were eating of the gold in
Hispaniola.

During the day we traded with some of the
Indians for gold nuggets which we intended to
take to Queen Isabella. The men were

encouraged to know that we were near a very large gold mine.

Christmas Night I was alone for awhile in the ship's cabin and again I prayed that God would reveal His will. This time I received an answer. I immediately called a conference of the leaders from both the *Santa Maria* and the *Pinta*.

"Men," I declared, as I paced before them, "I have been much distressed by the wreck of the *Santa Maria*. I felt it was the greatest disaster that could have befallen us." I paused for a moment to give the men time to reflect on this.

"But, I am convinced now that it was the will of God," I continued. "I believe the Lord has ordained this shipwreck because He has selected this place for a settlement."

The men were surprised at this announcement.

"So, I am calling for volunteers who will stay here while we sail back to Spain for more supplies and men."

"What about protection, Admiral?" one of the men asked. "What if the Caribs should come?"

We had all heard about a tribe of warlike Indians, who ate human flesh. They sometimes invaded these islands. The local natives were terrified at even the mention of their name.

"We will build a fort for protection," I said. "Even the Caribs will not be able to harm you. The local natives are very friendly, and wish to cooperate with us."

The men were pleased with the idea of a settlement. We had no trouble getting volunteers to stay. After all, the climate in Hispaniola was perfect, the Indians were friendly, and there was enough food and stores to last for at least a year. In addition, there was the prospect of striking it rich by finding the gold mine Guacanagari had told us about.

"I will stay and supervise the building of the settlement," volunteered Alonso Morales, the *Santa Maria's* carpenter.

"And I will help build the settlement!" volunteered Diego Perez.

I appointed Diego de Harana, the cousin of my wife Beatriz, to command the fort in my absence. I named the fort *La Navidad* because it was on Christmas Day that God ordained it should be built.

Thirty-nine men volunteered to stay at the fort. We used the timbers from the wrecked *Santa Maria* to build it. In the hugh cellar we stored the provisions for the men.

On January 2, 1493, we had a farewell party and invited Guacanagari and some of his Indians. He and I had become great friends by this time. He shed tears at the thought of my leaving. I assured him, however, that I would be back and we would renew our friendship.

We had hoped to sail at once, but the winds did not cooperate. It was not until sunrise on January 6 that we were finally able to weigh anchors and move away from Fort Navidad.

I was surprised that morning to see the *Pinta* running down the coastline. So, Martin Pinzon, who had deserted even his own brother, was coming back.

Naturally, I was furious at Martin for what he had done, but I tried to have a forgiving spirit as I felt my Lord would desire. I did demand that he release four men and two girls he had captured, and told him that we were homeward bound. We anchored the following day near another island and for the first time encountered Indians with weapons of their own. They were armed with bows and arrows and a mild skirmish followed when the Indians fired at some of our men. No one was seriously hurt. We finally weighed anchors for the last time in these strange lands and headed north by east to pick up the prevailing winds that would take us home to Spain.

The winds were strong and soon our little ships were moving steadily toward the east.

"Now I know what you meant, Master," said Pedro one day, "when you said we would find the winds to take us home."

Pedro was excited about going home. "I can hardly wait," he said, "to tell my friends about all the exciting things we have seen!"

Martin Pinzon and the *Pinta* were way out ahead of us. I made no effort to keep together. I had determined that I would have nothing more to do with such a man.

The crew was happy. We continued to worship the Lord who had blessed us so richly. The men and boys delighted in singing the hymns and in the times of prayer. There was much joy aboard the little ship *Nina*. After all, we were homeward bound, and my heart longed to see my family and friends.

The winds carried us on. What a joy it was to feel the sensation of moving so swiftly through the waters. Vincente Pinzon, Peralonzo Nino, and I had a joyous time each day plotting the course of the ship and charting the progress.

"At the rate we are going, we will be home much sooner than we expected," said a pleased Vincente one day as we went over the charts.

"The sooner the better," cried Pedro. "I'm anxious to see my friends."

On Monday, February 12 a storm began. At first, the seas began to swell and great waves pounded the ship. The winds increased throughout the day and by nightfall the ship was rolling and pitching in the angry seas.

For days the storm raged and torrential rains poured down upon us. We could not rest, but had to keep at our jobs night and day to save the ship and our lives.

"Master, you must get some rest," said Pedro. He tugged at my sleeves, trying to persuade me to return to the cabin.

"We must pray, Pedro," I said. "Call the men together."

We met in the hold of the ship. While the storm raged around us we prayed and sincerely made promises to our Lord if He would but save us.

After the prayers there was a lull in the storm. But that night it broke loose again. It seemed that any moment the ship would be dashed to pieces and all of us would perish. The ship rose and fell in the violent seas.

In the cabin alone I wrote a long letter to King Ferdinand and Queen Isabella. I outlined for them my voyage, and told them of the strange new lands discovered. I wrapped the parchment letter in a waxed cloth to protect it from water, and ordered one of our men to seal it up in a large wooden cask and to cast it into the sea. It was my hope that if we should perish at sea, someone would find the letter in the cask and deliver it to Our Majesties. That way, the king and queen would know that I had been faithful to my mission, and they could claim the lands which I had already claimed for them.

Meanwhile, I continued praying that God's will would be done. I knew that He had sustained me through many storms before. I prayed that He might lead me through this one.

Shortly after sunrise on the following day, although there was no sun to be seen, one of the sailors named Ruy Garcia sighted land dead

ahead. There was much excitement aboard the
ship as we tried to determine what land it was.

"I believe it is Castile itself," cried Garcia.
"The Lord has answered our prayers and brought
us directly home out of the storm."

"No, it couldn't be Castile," insisted Vincente
Pinzon. "It must be Madeira."

"What do you think it is, Admiral?" Vincente
asked me.

"I believe it is one of the Azores," I replied,
"probably Santa Maria, the southern-most island."

The next day we searched the northern side of
the island for a suitable place to anchor. I sent the
boat ashore with some men to talk to the natives.
They confirmed my belief that we were in the
Azores. The island was Santa Maria, one of the
smallest islands in the Azores. The people of the
island said they had never seen such a tempest as
there had been for the past fifteen days. They
marveled at the fact that we had managed to stay
afloat.

I knew we might be in danger because the
Azores were ruled by the Portuguese, and we
were, of course, flying the Spanish flag. But when
the men reported the friendliness of the people, I
felt more at ease.

Finally, a delegation from the island came out to
the ship. They brought us fresh chickens, a real
delicacy to one who had been eating sourdough
biscuits for so long! I asked them about their
religion, and they replied that there was a small
chapel on the island.

I was anxious to fulfill the vows we had made to
the Lord when the storm was raging. So I sent half
the crew into the village with instructions for them
to visit the chapel and offer prayers of
thanksgiving. When they had finished, they were

to return to the ship while the rest of us went into town to offer our prayers.

When the men did not return, I became suspicious of foul play. I ordered the ship moved to another spot off shore where we might have time to decide what to do. While we were moving the ship, we noticed a group of Portuguese soldiers, fully armed, launching a boat to come out to our ship.

We anchored the ship and prepared for a battle if necessary. The boat, however, moved next to ours. The governor of the island, who said he knew me, although I did not know him, tried to persuade me to come aboard.

I refused to do this, feeling that it was a trap designed to capture me. Instead, I invited the governor, Joao de Castanheira, to come aboard the *Nina* for our discussion.

He refused to do this and actually told me of his contempt for the Sovereigns of Spain. I, in turn, threatened to send my men ashore to invade the island if my men were not released immediately. How I expected to do this with only sixteen men, I do not know. But I was angry at the way things were going and determined that I would not allow an upstart Portuguese governor to prevent me from getting home.

When the governor realized that I would refuse to enter his trap, he retreated with his men to the island. After conferring with other officials, he decided to release our men. They told us later they were seized while they were in the chapel praying!

Three days out from the Azores, on our last leg home, we ran into another storm. It seemed that fate, or the Devil himself, was determined that we would never make it. Again the storm raged, and the little ship *Nina* was tossed about by the winds. We prayed again, this time desperately. We wanted to get home so badly.

At last, on March 3, we spotted in the distance the coastline of Europe. But I recognized immediately we were still in trouble. I had sailed into the port of Lisbon enough times to know that familiar scenery. We already knew from our experience in the Azores what trouble the Portuguese could give us. Now we were sailing directly into their chief port!

As soon as we had anchored outside the city of Lisbon, I sent by dispatch a letter to King Ferdinand which I had written at sea. The letter in part said:

> *Sire,*
>
> *I know that you will be pleased at the great success with which Our Lord had blessed my voyage. . . . I sailed from the Canary Islands to the Indies in thirty-three days with the ships you, the King and Queen, our Sovereigns, gave to me. I found there many islands filled with a great number of people. I have taken possession of all of them in the name of Your Highnesses.*

While we were repairing our ship at Lisbon, I was invited by King John of Portugal to come for an interview. This time I took some of the Indians we had brought back with us and marched triumphantly to the castle.

I was worried at first. I knew the treachery of King John. He had sent an expedition out behind my back, and had refused my offers time after time to find the Indies for Portugal. What was to prevent him from killing me, capturing the *Nina*, and sending another expedition to claim the islands for Portugal?

My fears were relieved, however, when he received me. He was pleased to see the Indians, proof enough that I had not been encroaching on his territories in Africa. I gave him an account of my voyage. I could tell with delight that he was sorry he had not listened to me many years before.

Back aboard the *Nina* at last, with a good northeastern wind blowing, we lifted anchor and sailed out of the harbor of Lisbon.

"We are going home at last, Pedro!" I said to my cabin boy.

Pedro was excited. He turned a complete flip on the deck as the sailors joined in the gaiety.

On the fifteenth day of March, we sighted the Saltes River shortly after daybreak. We were forced to tack our sails and hold back, waiting for the tide that would take us into the harbor. The tide finally began rolling in about noon and the *Nina* slipped across the bar and eased up the river toward Palos. It had been two hundred and twenty-four days, exactly thirty-two weeks, since we left, and all of us were glad to be home.

Later that afternoon, while getting things in order so we could leave the ship, Peralonso Nino came bursting into my cabin.

"Look, Admiral!" he said excitedly. "Look who's coming in on the same tide as we are."

I looked out the window of the cabin. There was no mistake about it. Martin Pinzon and the *Pinta* were behind us. The flags of Spain were waving proudly in the breeze.

tROUBLE In
the neW WORLD

The king and queen had moved their court to Barcelona. They moved about more than any other monarchs in Europe. I dispatched a second letter from Palos, just in case my first letter had been lost. The mail service in Spain was very bad, and it took weeks for my letter to be delivered and a reply to be received.

I spent those weeks at La Rabida praying and celebrating with the men. Father Antonio was good to me, seeing that special dishes were prepared to my taste, and making me comfortable. I needed the rest, because the voyage to the Indies had aggravated my arthritis. There were days when I could hardly move from the pain and stiffness.

On Easter Sunday the reply came. My heart overflowed as I read the letter from the king and queen. They wanted me to come immediately to Barcelona to make a report of my voyage.

By this time the news of my voyage and

discoveries had been flashed all across Spain. I was treated as a hero by masses of people who crowded the roads to see us pass.

The procession was a long one. I rode in front, this time on a magnificent horse. Following me were some of the men who had sailed with me. Behind them came the strange Indians, naked except for a girdle of beads around their waists. We also carried cages with parrots and other strange birds from the new lands.

By the time we reached Cordova the crowds were excited to a fever pitch. Nothing like this had ever been seen in Spain before.

"Look, Mother!" I heard one little boy in the crowd exclaim. "There is *Don* Christopher Columbus, the hero of all Spain!"

I had obeyed God and become a Christ-Bearer. The crowds looked and gawked as we rode triumphantly into the city where Beatriz and my two sons were waiting for me. Beatriz was lovelier than ever. She greeted me with a kiss.

"And who is this handsome young man you have with you?" I asked, as Diego, my son, smiled broadly.

"I am twelve years old now, Father," Diego reminded me.

"Yes, I know," I replied. "And you have grown very tall!"

Little Ferdinand was four years old. He looked about him at the excitement and hardly knew what was happening.

"Will you stay with us long, Chris?" asked Beatriz. "We have missed you so much."

"I am sorry," I said. "But I must move on to Barcelona to report to the king and queen. After that, while I am waiting for the second voyage to begin I will have time to visit my family."

"I want to go with you, Father, when you sail again," begged Diego.

"We will see, my son," I said.

It was a great distance across Spain to Barcelona. It took us many days to get there. Some of the days it was raining, but the crowds still lined the roads to watch the strange procession as we made our way slowly across the land.

The king and queen received us in their castle. There was much ceremony and pomp as we marched into the hugh reception hall. Trumpets were blaring. Crowds stood in the balcony and cheered.

I bowed and kissed the hands of the king and queen. To my amazement and delight they invited me to sit next to them on the throne as we reviewed the voyage.

I told them of our sailing the seas and of the strange lands God had allowed us to discover.

"Did you find China or Cipangu?" the king asked.

"No, Your Majesty," I replied. "I feel certain that we were near them. But we did find many islands. One of them, which I named Hispaniola, is a large island with much gold and precious metals."

"That's quite amazing," said the king. "And these natives you brought back, are they from Hispaniola?"

"They are, Your Highness," I said. "They have been very valuable to us as guides and interpreters. We intend to baptize them into the Christian faith."

Queen Isabella was pleased that I had not forgotten my vows to take our religion to the heathen.

"On your next voyage, *Don* Columbus," she

said, "you must take some missionaries who can help these people find Christ."

We were already planning to sail again, this time with a fleet of seventeen vessels. I wanted to take with me all the supplies the men would need in the settlement at La Navidad. We even planned to take horses for the first time to the New World.

I spent several weeks at the court of the king and queen, celebrating with them the Holy Services of the season. I also made a long journey to Guadalupe to fulfill the religious promises I had made aboard the *Nina* during the storm at sea. It was here that real peace was restored to my soul. I made a new commitment to take missionaries with me to the Indies to convert the heathen to Christ.

I had learned on my first voyage that most of my time had to be taken up with the administration of the affairs of the ships under my command and the exploration of new lands. I sensed already that I lacked the time to actually do much witnessing for Jesus, although I used every opportunity I could find to share my faith in Jesus with others.

I knew I would need missionaries who were trained in the Scripture and could witness. They could devote their full time and energies to converting the Indians in the New World. I was not shirking my responsibility as a Christ-Bearer. I simply felt that my primary responsibility was to discover new lands so that others might take the Gospel to the people there. The queen had confirmed this idea by her suggestion that I take trained missionaries with me on the next voyage.

Finally, when I had finished at Guadalupe, I had a little time to spend with my family at Cordova. Beatriz had sad news for me however, when I arrived. She had received the news from my brother Diego. He was now a young clergyman as we had dreamed he would be.

"Your mother and your brother, Giovanni, both died while you were at sea," Beatriz told me with tears in her eyes.

For a moment I could not speak. It had been such a long time since I had seen my mother. But I thought of her often. Through the years Bartholomew and I had sent her money, both for herself, and to pay for Diego's education.

"And Father?" I asked. "Is he well?"

"Yes," replied Beatriz. "Your father is well. Your sister, Bianca, is married and lives close by to care for him."

"And Diego?" I asked.

"Diego is still in training and very excited about all the news he has been hearing about you." Beatriz smiled as she continued telling me the family news.

"I must write Diego and ask him to sail on my next voyage," I said. "I need him to help convert the Indians."

"And what about Bartholomew?" Beatriz asked.

"Oh, I have already written that rascal," I stated. "I need Bartholomew very badly to help govern the new settlement in the Indies."

After many months of preparation we were ready to sail. We had no trouble enlisting a crew this time. People from all over Spain wanted to sail with *Don* Christopher Columbus to the mysterious lands of the Indies. We were forced to turn down many who wanted to go. Over one thousand and two hundred people were signed up to sail on the seventeen vessels. Among these were twelve missionaries, in addition to my brother, Diego. The missionaries were placed in charge of Father Bernard Buil.

The supplies were much harder to obtain. I was determined to carry with me every thing that was needed by the colonists in the new land. This included food, firearms, seeds, plants, animals, and tools of a great assortment. It took us months to gather all these items.

Finally, we were ready to sail on September 24, 1493. There was only one thing wrong. I paced the deck of the flagship and looked eagerly into the faces of the crowd that had gathered in Cadiz to watch our departure.

"There is no sign of Bartholomew," I said to Diego. "We have waited as long as we can. We must sail without him."

"Perhaps he did not receive your letter," Diego said. "I have heard that the mail system in France is as bad as it is in Spain."

"I hope that is the case," I muttered sadly. "I would hate to know that anything bad had happened to him."

I looked at Diego in his long, black robe and knew that I would have to depend on him to govern the men while I explored. I peered over the railing of the ship as long as I could, hoping that Bartholomew would come at the last moment.

The crowd in Cadiz went wild when we weighed the anchors, and one by one, began to move the ships out to sea. They cheered and waved flags while the trumpets sounded, and cannons boomed.

I stood with Diego under the flapping sails of my new flagship, a new *Santa Maria*, much larger and more sail-worthy than the old one. I was dressed in my new Admiral's uniform, complete with embroidered sleeves and sequined collar. I waved my hat to the crowds on the shore who shouted, "*Don* Columbus! *Don* Columbus!"

"This voyage is much different from the first one," I said to Alonso de Hojeda, one of the young caballeros on this new voyage. "On the first voyage we had only a few to cheer. No one believed we would discover anything."

"But now it is different," Hojeda said. "You are widely acclaimed, and all of Spain believes."

We made our way down the coast to the Canaries. We stopped in Gromera for a few days while fresh food was loaded aboard the ships. I paid a courtesy call on *Dona* Beatriz. From Gromera we picked up the westerly winds and sailed across the Atlantic.

The crews were joyous and happy. This time we knew where we were going. There was much gaiety aboard the ships as the prevailing winds and calm seas carried us forth to the New World.

On Saturday, November 2, I sensed we were near land. I ordered a shortening of the sails and lookouts posted. All day the men anxiously peered ahead, searching for land.

The next morning we heard a shout from a crew member on the forecastle of the *Santa Maria*, "Land ahead!" The men began to cheer as we saw before us the unmistakable outline of an island.

The first island we spotted I named *Dominica*, in honor of the Lord's Day, Sunday. We sailed along through a maze of islands which later became known as the Leeward Islands.

Luis, one of the young sailors who had been on the first voyage, stood on the deck as we watched the islands go by.

"I believe you have discovered the fastest route possible to the Indies, Sir," he remarked. "On the first voyage we sailed for thirty-three days, but on this one we made it in twenty-one!"

"Yes," I replied. "I believe the more southerly route is best."

In the evening of November 4, I ordered the fleet to anchor off the island which I had named *Santa Maria de Guadalupe* (Guadalupe). Here I fulfilled a promise I had made at Guadalupe in Spain during my pilgrimage there.

Diego Marquez took a company of ten men ashore to see what they could find. They went into the interior of the island and became lost. We were forced to wait six days while a searching party went to look for them. What they found on the island was a tribe of Caribs — cannibals who made a practice of eating human flesh. In one deserted village they found captive Indian children who were being fattened up for a feast. They also found bones and pieces of human flesh where the Caribs had been cooking their meals.

Needless to say, we were all happy when the men were safely aboard ship and the orders were given to sail away.

Working our way to the northwest, we continued to sight many islands, all of them beautiful and serene in the sea. We made no further excursions on the islands however, because all of us were anxious to visit La Navidad.

We arrived in Hispaniola after sunset on November 27. Our spirits were still high. We expected a shore party to spot us quickly and come out to greet us. We fired one of the guns on the *Santa Maria* and waited. But nothing happened. There was only silence.

"What do you think is wrong?" asked Diego. We peered into the darkness toward the island.

"I don't know," I answered. "I only hope nothing has happened to the brave men at La Navidad."

"I can't imagine why the men are not here," Luis joined in. "They surely must be anxious for some good Spanish food."

"Shall we move the fleet in closer, Admiral?" asked the pilot.

"No," I commanded. "I remember what happened to the first *Santa Maria*. The reefs along the shore are very treacherous. We will simply have to wait until morning."

We spent a sleepless night fretting about the men at La Navidad. As soon after daylight as possible we moved the fleet in closer to the shore. I sent a shore party out to see what was wrong. They returned shortly to report that the fort had been burned to the ground. There was no sign of the thirty-nine brave men we had left in the New World.

The news shocked all of us on the ships. But I determined to find out what had happened. I took a few brave men and went into the forest looking for my Indian friend Guacanagari.

I found him in a squalid Indian village. He was sick, and at first refused to see me. But I insisted, and shortly I was ushered into his tent.

Guacanagari told me that several Indian tribes had rebelled against our men because of their cruelty to the Indians. One day they stormed the settlement and massacred everyone. Guacanagari had tried to help, but he was unable to stop the warring Indians.

"I believe my friend Guacanagari," I said to Diego. "There is nothing for us to do but rebuild the settlement."

"What about your exploration?" Diego asked. He knew I was anxious to sail further west.

"I will explore while you stay here and build the new settlement. You will be governor while I am gone," I instructed Diego.

"I will do the best I can," Diego promised. "I only wish Bartholomew was here to help." he added.   I sensed that he dreaded the great responsibility I had given him.

"You will do fine, Diego," I assured him. "I am sure Bartholomew will be here someday."

I singled out Alonso Hojedo and commissioned him as captain of the army to explore the gold mine.

"But I want you to understand," I said. "I am leaving my brother Diego as governor in my stead. I expect you and your men to cooperate with him and give him your support."

"Admiral, why don't we build the new settlement near the river so we will have fresh water and be closer to the gold mines," he suggested.

"That's an excellent idea," I said. "I will expect you and your men to help build the settlement before you start looking for gold."

Leaving the new settlement in the hands of Diego and Hojeda, I boarded the *Santa Maria* and sailed away. I wanted to find all that I could in the New World, and I knew my time was getting short.

searching for the mainland

The new settlement in Hispaniola was named *Isabella* in honor of our queen. Now that it was under way, and Diego and Hojeda were there to build it, I felt it was time to continue looking for the mainland.

I felt confused and disappointed about my discoveries. According to what I had read, and the maps of the world that were available to us, I should have found China, Japan, and India. But so far, all I had discovered was many islands. These were all beautiful and interesting, but they were not what we had expected.

I knew also that the king and queen would be unhappy with our mission. In the first place, they were expecting gold from the new lands, which so far, we had not found. They were looking too, for a profitable trade route to the lands of the Orient, and that we had not found.

On April 24, 1494, I left Isabella with three ships. I used the *Nina* as my flagship, and the two caravels, *San Juan*, and *Cordera*, to haul supplies and to help with the exploration.

We sailed west by north to the land of Colba (Cuba) where we had been before. I was not yet convinced this was an island. I believed at the time it was part of the mainland and I wanted to explore it further.

The natives of Colba received us in a friendly way and prepared for us dishes of fish and iguana. But the Indian interpreters we had brought with us from Hispaniola were unable to understand the language of these strange Indians.

One day while we were sailing along the coast of Colba we saw ahead of us majestic mountains which seemed to rise up out of the sea. We ran down to this new island which I thought was the most beautiful one I had discovered. The island was Jamaica, and it was heavily populated with Indians. The native canoes on Jamaica were the largest we had seen. Some of them were at least 96 feet long. They were hewn from the giant mahogany trees from the forests of Jamaica.

We sailed back to Colba soon however, because I wanted so badly to find the mainland. We threaded our ships in and out of the many cays and coves of the coastline, moving westward on the south side of Colba.

Everywhere there were strange animals and creatures we had not seen before. Fernando de Luna, one of the men on the *Nina*, first spotted the flamingo birds with their bright colors and long legs which looked like sticks. Then we discovered a new method of fishing which amazed our men beyond measure.

The natives used a tame fish, called the *remora* (sucking fish) to catch other fish. They attached a line to the tails of these fish and allowed them to swim alongside their boats. The remora fish would swim ahead and attach itself to a larger fish, or a turtle. The natives would then haul them in. Truly a remarkable way to catch fish!

For almost five months we sailed in and out of the islands. We returned to Jamaica and discovered a new island called Puerto Rico. But two things happened which caused us to turn back.

First, I collapsed aboard the *Nina* from complete exhaustion. The long months of constant work, kedging the ships in and out of harbors, and directing them through the shallow waters, had completely exhausted me.

Secondly, the ships themselves were in need of repairs. The eighty men on the three ships were cheered by the news that we were returning to Isabella.

"Even the small comforts of that place will be better than this," remarked one of the sailors. He was really homesick for Spain.

Reluctantly, I gave the orders to turn back. I still believed that we had spotted the mainland. But I was not absolutely sure. Where were the cities Marco Polo had talked about? And the houses with roofs made of gold? All we had seen were shabby Indian villages. They had no houses, only tents, and the natives, although friendly, were far from being civilized. I could not explain the mystery of all of this.

We sailed around the island of Jamaica once more on our way home. This time, one of the Indian chiefs, together with his wife and two beautiful daughters, came out to the ship in a boat and talked with us in sign language. The chief wanted me to take him and his family back to Spain. I declined to do this, but promised to visit them again when we returned.

On September 29 our little fleet sailed into the river bed at Isabella. We had been gone five months, and it was good to be home again. When I stepped on land, a small party of men from the settlement was waiting. I thought I saw a familiar face in the crowd, but I wasn't sure until he stepped up close to me.

"Bartholomew!" I cried. "How in the world did you get here?"

"I missed your boat by one day, Brother Chris," he said. "But when I talked to the queen about it, she decided to send three more caravels with supplies for the settlement. I sailed with them. So, here I am in the New World you have discovered."

"Then you have been here for some time," I said.

"Yes," replied Bartholomew. "I have been here for three months waiting for your return."

Diego was happy to see me, too. He had had great difficulties with the settlement after I left, but things had been better since Bartholomew had arrived.

"Tell me about the progress of the settlement," I said to Diego after awhile.

"There isn't much to tell about its progress," he replied sadly. "But I have much to tell you."

I looked around the settlement. I could see that not much had been done. The buildings were only half completed, everything was scattered about. The sacks of seeds we had brought from Spain were still rotting on the ground.

"We will tell you all about it, Chris," Bartholomew interrupted. "But first you must go to bed. The men tell me that you have been very sick at sea. You do not look well at all."

I knew Bartholomew was right. Even as I stood there I became dizzy, and I was so weak my legs could hardly bear me up. The pains of my arthritis were hurting me too. I returned to my cabin on the *Nina*, which was the most comfortable place I could find, and went to bed.

For days I was unable even to walk. My meals were prepared and brought to me in the cabin. Gradually I began to regain my strength.

Diego talked to me about the problems at Isabella. I learned that Hojeda and others had given him much trouble in my absence.

"He left immediately after you did," reported Diego. "He refused to help with the settlement. All he could think of was finding the gold and mistreating the Indians."

"Did he find any gold?" I asked. I knew the king and queen were expecting lots of gold from the new settlement.

"He found some," reported Diego. "That is the only good news we have had since you left."

It was Bartholomew who told me about the disgruntled settlers who had returned to Spain.

"It was a group headed by the soldier named Margarite," he said. "They were not happy with the way things were going here so they took some ships and sailed back to Spain."

"Father Buil was in that group, too," reported Diego.

"Father Buil?" I asked. "What was he unhappy about?"

"He did not like my administration," Diego said sadly. "He told me he would report all the bad things he had seen here to the king and queen."

"Well, perhaps it is best he is gone." I said. "To tell you the truth, I never did really understand him."

"I didn't either," said Diego. "But I am afraid he will cause us much trouble with the king and queen."

Shortly after I returned to Isabella a fleet of four vessels arrived from Spain with fresh provisions for the colony. The fleet was commanded by Antonio de Torres. He personally delivered to me a letter from the king and queen.

I searched the letter for any sign of displeasure that might have resulted from the reports of the disgruntled colonists who had returned to Spain. But there was none. In fact, the Sovereigns thanked me for the good work I had done and for my enterprise "which for the most part has come true just as if you had seen it before you spoke about it."

The letter also spoke of a new treaty which the king and queen had signed with Portugal. They wanted my opinion on the treaty and wondered if I could return to Spain and discuss it with them. The letter stated however, that if I could not return, I could send my brother, or someone else in authority, to express my views to them.

I knew when I read the letter that I should return to Spain. But the illness which had kept me in bed for almost five months was still with me. I feared the voyage. I sent Diego back to Spain with my report. He was to tell the king and queen that I would return as soon as I was able.

Meanwhile, work in the settlement began to improve. Gradually my strength and health returned, and I busied myself with the details of administration.

Bartholomew was a great help to me. I had appointed him governor of the island. He was a strong and capable leader who could handle the men well. Soon crops were planted, and we had fresh vegetables daily. Buildings were erected, including the first church in the New World.

I remember the joy I experienced on the first Sunday that we worshiped in the church. It was a joyous occasion because many of the Indians who had been converted worshiped with us. I had at least seen some results of my role as Christ-Bearer in the conversions of these heathen. There would be many more conversions in the New World I was sure, as more lands were discovered and settled, and more missionaries came to tell the natives about Jesus.

In the Summer of 1495 the little settlement at Isabella was thriving. More settlers had arrived from Spain. Gold was being brought in from the mountains. The spirit of the people was good. It seemed that all of us were determined to make a go of it in the New World.

Then disaster struck. A wind with a force I had never seen before either on land or sea, struck the island of Hispaniola. The natives called it a *huracan* (hurricane). The wind uprooted giant trees and dashed three of our ships to pieces. Violent waves tore away trees from the land. The island was completely devastated. We were thankful God had spared our lives.

We had lost all our ships but one, the *Nina*. It would take us months to rebuild the settlement and get things back to normal again. I immediately ordered the men to build another ship because I knew I would have to sail to Spain soon for help.

The first ship built in the New World was a caravel which I named the *Santa Cruz*. While we were building the ship a new fleet arrived from Spain, bringing more supplies and more colonists. But they also brought bad news. The reports of Margarite and Father Buil had finally reached the king and queen, and they were very unhappy about the situation in the colony.

The king and queen had sent Juan de Aguado to the island to investigate our affairs. To make it worse, they had given him the authority to go over my head and speak directly to the people.

"I must return home at once," I said to Bartholomew. "Somehow, I will get to the bottom of this."

"What do you wish me to do?" asked Bartholomew, who was always anxious to help.

"You will stay here and govern the colony, and rebuild the settlement," I said.

We had already decided to build the new settlement in another location. We wanted to be away from the marshy lands of the river bed where there was no protection at all from the hurricanes.

"I will stay," said my faithful brother. "And with God's help I will build a new settlement."

"I've been thinking about that," I said. "Let's name the new settlement *San Domingo* in honor of our father."

It was March 10, 1496, before I was finally able to sail for Spain. We sailed in two small ships, the *Nina* and the *Santa Cruz*. On our way we revisited

Guadalupe where we stopped for fresh water. Soon afterwards we were on our way home.

When we sailed into the harbor at Cadiz, I found my old friend Peralonso Nino. He was preparing to sail to the colony with more provisions and supplies.

"How are things in the New World?" Peralonso asked.

I told Peralonso about the hurricane, the sickness, and the devastation of the island. I also told him about the new settlement that even then was being built by my brother Bartholomew and the colonists. I was surprised that he did not decide to stay in Spain. But he sailed away to the mysterious lands I had found in the sea.

The king and queen wrote me a letter inviting me to their court, which was now located in Burgos, all the way to the north across Spain. I could hardly wait to get there because I wanted to see my sons, Diego and Ferdinand, who were both serving as pages for *Don* Juan.

I reported to the king and queen. In spite of the reports I had received, they were very gracious to me. They received the gifts of gold nuggets which I presented to them with pleasure. I spent several days with them discussing the new colony and the other explorations I wanted to make in the New World.

"I will need at least eight ships," I told the queen one day in a private conversation. She spoke to me honestly and frankly.

"My husband, the king will not be very favorable to that proposal now," she said. "He has been very disturbed by the fact that your discoveries have cost us a great deal of money."

"But it will all be repaid someday, Your Highness," I assured her. "The enterprise will make Spain the richest nation in the world."

"Perhaps that is so," she replied. "I certainly hope so. But meanwhile, we must go slowly in our request for a new voyage. I am sure that the king will come around. But it will take some time."

"Whatever you think, Your Highness," I said. "I am at your service."

"And I still have faith in you, *Don* Columbus," said the queen. "I want you to know that."

The words of the queen sustained me for almost two years while I patiently waited for another fleet and another change. Meanwhile, I spent some busy days with my family. We had to catch up on all the things we had missed doing together.

BOUNÒ IN ChAINS

We sailed from Seville on May 30, 1498, with eight ships and three hundred settlers. It was good to be at sea again. The two long years of waiting for a third voyage to begin had made me restless and eager to be going.

We stopped at the island of Madeira where I visited with some members of the family of my beloved Felipa. Then, catching the trade winds we slipped away to the Canaries where we made our usual stop for more food and supplies.

At the Canary Islands we divided the fleet. I took three ships with me to sail south by west, and sent the others on the direct route to Hispaniola. I was anxious to continue my exploration. This time I wanted to find the continent I had been looking for on my other voyages.

After seventeen days of sailing one of our men on lookout shouted, "Land!" In the distance we could see an island with three distinct mountain peaks rising majestically up from the sea. I named the island *Trinidad* after the Holy Trinity. Since we needed fresh water, we decided to anchor near Trinidad and barter some with the natives.

The natives of Trinidad had lighter skin than the others we had seen in the Indies. They were graceful and handsome to look upon. Their long hair was worn straight, like the Spaniards of Castile. They wore scarves of cotton on their heads.

Our first meeting with them was not very pleasant. A canoe with about twenty-four men in it came rowing out to our ship. The men were armed with bows and arrows. They carried shields to protect them from attack.

When the boat would not come close to our ship, I asked one of the men to play his tambourine on the deck while other men danced. I hoped the festivities might interest the natives enough that they would come on out to the ship.

The plan backfired on us. Evidently, the Indians thought we were doing a war dance. They showered us with arrows which were swiftly projected from the bows in their boat. I ordered the ship's guns to fire over them. This frightened the natives, and they fled away without any real harm being done. Some of the men aboard ship had picked up their first souvenirs — Indian war arrows!

Sailing around to the southwestern end of Trinidad, we anchored in a narrow neck of water which I called the Serpent's Mouth. The current here was very swift. The land that lay to the west of us was not a part of the island. There were giant waves in the Serpent's Mouth, and I noticed that large amounts of fresh water were being pumped into the stream.

Exploring further, we found the mouth of a large river which surely could come only from great distances. The natives called their land *Paria*

(Venezuela). They had named the river the *Orinoco*.

"What do you make of it, Admiral?" the pilot of the ship asked me.

"I believe we have discovered the mainland," I said. "The large amount of fresh water in the sea means the river must be a very long one, stretching far into the continent itself."

The natives of Paria told us of the pearl fisheries nearby. They said the ocean bed was literally covered with pearls. It was here, near the river bed of the Orinoco, that Europeans first stepped ashore on the new continent (South America).

I was sure this was part of the mainland. But the mainland of what? It was not China, nor India. It was evidently some new land, which no one had dreamed even existed. I did not know at this time how extensive a discovery we had made. Later, I was to learn that we were on a part of a vast new continent, unknown to the civilized world before!

At that moment we all knew we had a great discovery, but we were not sure what it was. I was thankful to God for His blessings, and I claimed the land for Spain.

Shortly after our discoveries near Trinidad we sailed for San Domingo. I was anxious to see how the settlement was coming and to send the news of our new discoveries to Spain.

It was good to see Bartholomew and Diego again, but I noticed that the settlement was only half completed. After two and a half years very little progress had been made.

The trouble had begun shortly after I sailed home to Spain. Bartholomew told me about it.

"Francisco Roldan, the man you appointed as chief justice before you left, rebelled against us. He took about seventy men from the settlement and went off to live in the southwestern corner of

Hispaniola. He actually set up a rival kingdom there. We have had nothing but trouble."

"Besides that," complained Diego, "we are out of food."

"But what about the supply ships I send to you?" I asked.

"Unfortunately," said Bartholomew, "they landed on the side of the island that is controlled by Roldan. He got most of the supplies. Two of the ships finally came over here, and I have managed to get most of the men from Roldan's grasp. But most of the supplies were lost."

"What about Hojeda?" I asked. I remembered the trouble he had been before.

"Hojeda has returned to Spain," Diego reported. "It was a good riddance, too."

Later Bartholomew confessed to me. "Perhaps I have been too harsh with the men. Now that you are here, maybe you can help us straighten out the revolt."

I began by writing a letter to Roldan. I offered amnesty to all the men who had rebelled and guaranteed them a safe return to Spain if they would lay down their arms and stop fighting. My aim was to restore peace to the island so we could get on with the business of building a settlement.

After long months of negotiations we finally ended the revolt, and I restored Roldan to his office as chief justice. Many of the men who had rebelled with him returned to Spain safely as I had promised.

When peace was restored, I felt it was time to build the settlement in earnest. I personally supervised some of the building projects and helped the men with their problems. Soon, things began to happen. Buildings were completed. Crops were sown in the fertile soil, and a spirit of cooperation filled the air. The people became

excited about the possibilities that existed in the
New World. Many people were allowed to farm
individual plots of land and to claim that land for
themselves.

Just when things were beginning to blossom
again in San Domingo, more trouble developed.
First, there was another small rebellion. I sent
Bartholomew into the jungles with a small army to
put down the rebellion. I went off to Vega Real,
the area of the gold mine, to see how things were
progressing there. I left Diego in San Domingo to
keep the work going.

On August 23, 1499, a small fleet of ships sailed
into the harbor at San Domingo. In that fleet was
a man named Francisco de Bobadilla who
immediately took over the affairs of the island. He
introduced himself as the new governor, sent by
the king and queen to replace me, and to
straighten out the affairs of the colony.

The word was sent to me by messenger that I
should return to San Domingo with haste. It took
three days travel through the jungles to get there.
When I arrived, I found that Bobadilla had placed
Diego in jail and had taken over my private
quarters. He had confiscated everything that
belonged to me.

When I confronted him he explained his powers
to me.

"The king and queen have appointed me as
governor of Hispaniola," he said. "They have
given me absolute authority to return to Spain
anyone whom I deem necessary in order to restore
peace to the island."

Bobadilla stopped long enough to flail at a
mosquito buzzing around his head. Then he
continued.

"Therefore, *Don* Columbus, I am arresting you
and your brothers by order of the king and queen

and returning you to Spain to report your actions to the crown."

With that, Bobadilla ordered that I be placed in chains. None of the men would do the distasteful job of placing the chains upon me. Finally, Espinosa, my cook, stepped forward and volunteered to do it. He riveted the chains on my arms and legs, and I was carried away to a jail cell.

I received word that my brother, Bartholomew, had heard about my arrest and was preparing to march with his men against Bobadilla. Good old Bart! He was willing to risk his life to free me!

I persuaded him by messenger not to do this. I asked him instead to surrender to Bobadilla. I felt that Bobadilla had overstepped his authority and that justice would be done when we returned to Spain.

In a few days Bartholomew returned to San Domingo and quietly surrendered to Bobadilla. He was placed in chains and locked up in jail with Diego and me.

The humiliation of my arrest overwhelmed me. I could not believe it was happening. Here I was, Christopher Columbus, Admiral of the Ocean Sea, who had discovered and given to the king and queen vast territories which would make them the richest monarchs in history. And I was to be bound in chains and sent home like a common criminal.

Was this gratitude? Who could justify such action against one who had done so much for them? I prayed in my prison cell that God would forgive them for their acts of cruelty and humiliation to me and my brothers.

Finally, we were placed on two ships for the return to Spain. Diego and I were on one ship and Bartholomew on the other. As soon as the ships were out of the harbor, Andres Martin, the captain, and Alonso de Vallejo, the guard, came to me.

"Admiral," said Vallejo, "we wish to strike the chains from you."

"Why?" I asked.

"Because we do not believe the king and queen authorized Bobadilla to put you in chains," Andres said.

"Everyone knows that the accusations against you are false," Vallejo added.

But I refused to permit them to remove the chains. "I will wait," I said, "and see what the king and queen say about this."

Diego was freed from his chains however, and allowed to wait upon me. He was a great comfort and solace to me in this, the darkest hour of my life.

"I cannot believe the king and queen did this," he said to me one day. "It was the evil mind of Bobadilla who thought this up."

"I hope you are right, Diego," I said. "I had always believed that the king and queen, especially the queen, had great confidence in me. But now, I am beginning to wonder."

We spent the days on the long voyage home praying for God's guidance and deliverance. Even then, I was thinking of another trip to the Indies. I needed to find those pearls for the king and queen. I was sure there were still other lands, as yet undiscovered and uncharted, which I could find. And I still dreamed of opening up vast new areas for the Gospel of Christ so that millions of people who had never heard of Him might be converted. I might be in chains for the moment, but I still felt God's hand upon me. I knew my work was not yet finished.

We arrived in Cadiz in October. There were crowds of people in Cadiz to meet us. The word had gone out that the man who had opened up a whole new world for Spain was coming home in chains.

The crowds lined the roads from Cadiz to Seville to see the spectacle of the great hero being led along by guards with chains on his feet and hands. The popular reaction to this sight was overwhelming. The crowds protested the action of the monarchs. Everywhere there were shouts, "Free him! Free him!"

Many of my friends wrote letters of protest to the officials. "Why?" they asked. "Why is the noble *Don* Columbus in chains? Why, he has opened up a whole new world for Spain. Is this anyway to show our gratitude?"

Furious and angry protests swept through the land. It was encouraging to know that the people were upset at our treatment. They demanded immediate action from the king and queen.

Meanwhile, I was lodged in the monastery at Seville, waiting for orders from the king and queen. It was almost a month before those orders came. They ordered my immediate release from the chains and asked me to report to them at Granada.

On December 17 at the Alhambra in Granada I fell on my knees before King Ferdinand and Queen Isabella. I asked them to forgive me for any wrong which I might have done.

They immediately pardoned me and my brothers and apologized for the treatment we had received.

The queen burst into tears when she saw the look of gratitude on my face. "It was never our intention," she said, "for you to be placed in chains, or even arrested."

"That's right *Don* Columbus," the king added. "*Senor* Bobadilla clearly overstepped his authority by such action. For that we will demand an accounting from him."

Later the king told me, "We do feel, *Don* Columbus, that it is necessary to turn the affairs of the colony over to someone else. We believe that you are valuable as an explorer, not as an administrator."

At least they were expecting me to sail again. That was good news, and I rejoiced in my heart that God still wanted to use me.

Our family celebrated the Christmas holidays together in Seville for the first time in years. With me were my brothers, Bartholomew and Diego, my two sons, Diego and Ferdinand, and Beatriz. In spite of our recent ordeal the atmosphere was light and gay.

"All of Spain is talking about your discoveries, Chris," Beatriz said.

"Yes, Father," joined in Diego. "They are saying that you have discovered a vast continent that will make Spain the richest and most powerful nation on earth!"

"I hear that other discoveries are being made, too," I said.

"Yes," Bartholomew joined the conversation. "I heard that an Italian by the name of Amerigo Vespucci has been in the areas you have already charted around Trinidad."

"Will you go to the New World again, Father?" asked Ferdinand.

"I certainly will," I said. "The king has already authorized another fleet for me."

"May I go with you this time, Father?" asked Ferdinand. "I want to write an account of your travels and discoveries."

I looked at my youngest son. He was only twelve years old and still just a lad. My mind went back to that day when I was ten years old. I remembered how I had longed to sail the seas even then.

"Why not?" I said to Ferdinand. "The sea has been good to me. Perhaps it will be good for you, too!"

maROONed
ON JAMAICA

"Ferdinand, you take care of your father, now. Be sure he gets plenty of rest and good food." Beatriz smiled as she gave our son these last minute instructions.

"I will, Mother," Ferdinand replied. "Uncle Bartholomew and I will take care of him."

"And take care of yourself, too!" Diego beamed as he placed his arm around his younger brother.

"I will, Diego," said Ferdinand. "I wish you were coming with us."

"I wish so, too," Diego sighed as he spoke. "But I must stay here and look after Father's affairs."

"Good-bye!" we both said at once as we left our family and made our way aboard the caravel. The men were ready to sail so I gave the order to proceed. The sails unfurled and glistened in the balmy sunshine. It was May 11, 1502, when the four caravels slipped out of the harbor at Cadiz for my fourth journey to the New World.

It had been two years since I had sailed, and again, I was anxious for the sea. I had spent those years in and out of the court, making preparations for a new voyage. I had also been working on a book about the prophecies of the Bible. I felt sure that many of the prophecies were coming true because of my discoveries.

In that *Book of Prophecy* I had set forth my belief that the discovery of the New World was a thing that must happen before the end of the world. I believed that God had ordained me to become the one who would open up vast new worlds for the spreading of the Gospel.

In one section of the book I related how God had used me by writing the following account:

> *"At this time I both read and studied all kinds of literature: cosmography, histories, chronicles, and philosophy and other arts, to which our Lord opened my mind unmistakably to the fact that it was possible to navigate from here to the Indies, and He evoked in me the will for the execution of it; and with this fire I came to Your Highnesses. All those who heard of my plan disregarded it mockingly and with laughter. All the sciences of which I spoke were of no profit to me nor the authorities in them; only in Your Highnesses my faith, and my stay. Who would doubt that this light did not come from the Holy Spirit, anyway as far as I am concerned, which comforted with rays of marvelous clarity and with its Holy and Sacred Scriptures."*

Later I wrote about my belief that I was ordained to fulfill the prophecies of the Bible.

> *"Our Redeemer said that before the consummation [end] of this world all that was written by the prophets is to be accomplished. The greatest part of the prophecies and*

[of] the Holy Scriptures is already finished.
"I said above that much remained for the completion of the prophecies, and I say that there are great things in the world, and I say that the sign is that Our Lord is hastening them; the preaching of this Gospel in so many lands, in recent times, tells it to me."

On this voyage I intended to find, if possible, a way through the straits of the mainland which would enable me to sail completely around the world and to discover whatever lands had not yet been reached for the Gospel of Jesus.

Bartholomew was with me, serving as captain of one of the caravels. I also had the services of Diego Mendez, one of the bravest men who ever sailed the seas. And of course, Ferdinand was with me. He was fourteen now, and full of life and energy.

He quickly won the respect of the men on the ship by working right along with them. At first, they were a little wary of the Admiral's son. But when I heard one of the men yelling to Ferdinand, "Come on, lad, throw me that line! We haven't got all day!" I knew he had been accepted.

We sailed from the Canary Islands, after making our usual visit, and for twenty-one sun-drenched days we skimmed along through the sparkling waters of the Atlantic. The mood of the voyage was joyous. We expected to make more great discoveries. The men were looking forward to finding the pearl fisheries. I wanted to find the straits that would take us around the world.

We sighted land and discovered another beautiful island which I called *Martinique.* We intended to explore this region, but one of the ships in our fleet had developed a leak. I decided we had better go to San Domingo and see if we could get another ship.

"I don't know about that, Chris," said my brother Bartholomew, as we discussed the situation. "You know the queen asked us to stay away from there because she wanted to avoid any trouble."

"Yes," I remarked sadly. "But this is an emergency. Surely the queen did not mean to deny us the right to seek our own safety."

I suppose I should have listened to Bart. But there is a stubborn streak in most of us, and I happen to have one, too. I guess I resented, in a way, the queen's order not to go to Hispaniola. After all, I had discovered the island, helped build the settlement, and even owned a part of it according to my agreement with the crown. Surely I had the right to visit there if I wanted, especially in the case of an emergency.

So, I disregarded his advice and set our course for San Domingo. When we arrived I sent a boat to shore asking for permission to enter the harbor. When the boat returned, Mendez reported to me in my cabin.

"Admiral, there is a new governor on the island by the name of Ovando. He refused to grant you permission to enter the harbor."

I was humiliated and embarassed by his refusal, but I tried to conceal my feelings from Mendez.

"Did the governor give you any reason for his refusal?" I asked.

"No, he did not," reported Mendez.

"Did you ask him about another ship?" I inquired.

"I did, Admiral," said Mendez. "He said he was sorry, but every available ship he has is being loaded now for a trip to Spain. I inquired around and I learned that Bobadilla, Roldan, and Antonio de Torres are being sent home on the ships."

"You mean they are still on the island?" I asked.

"The new governor has only been here a short time," Mendez explained. "This is the first fleet sent home since he came."

Since we were not allowed the use of the harbor I moved the fleet further down the coast. I had noticed the giant dolphins of the sea were leaping higher into the air than they usually did. There was also a clammy calmness. I sensed that a storm was brewing.

I sent another message to Ovando warning him of a possible hurricane, and asking again for permission to seek safety from the storm in the harbor.

His reply was incredible. Again he refused permission to enter the harbor. He scoffed at the idea of a storm, saying that it couldn't possibly happen in beautiful weather like this. He informed me that the fleet was ready to sail the next day for Spain.

The fleet sailed on schedule. But it never reached Spain. The hurricane hit when they were only one day out from San Domingo. Only a few of them managed to creep back to safety. Bobadilla, Roldan, and Torres were all drowned in the sea.

We caught the fringe of the storm and sought safety in a cove. Fortunately, all four of our ships escaped without damage.

When the storm was over we repaired the leaking ship as best we could and sailed away to continue our exploration. We sailed past Jamaica in search of the continent (Central America).

We found the land, which we were sure was not an island, and began to work our way down the coast. The winds were against us most of the time. We were forced to tack our sails and move very cautiously along the marshy shores. At night we usually anchored the ships because of the danger of striking a reef.

The Indians in this area were far more advanced than any we had seen before. They wore cotton clothes, finely woven, and seemed to be more settled than the others we had seen.

Ferdinand was busy most of the time working on the ship with the men. But he found time to write down descriptions of all the fascinating animals and people we saw.

On August 17, Bartholomew and I went ashore close to a river (near present Panama Canal) and formally took possession of the land for the king and queen. I was sure, after talking with some of the natives in sign language, that we would find the strait we were looking for further south.

Pressing on, we came to another river which I named *Bethlehem*. Here I sent a group ashore to explore the area. They returned to report much gold in the area. They had found five mines within five leagues of the shore. The Indians had showed them from the top of a hill that more mines existed further on.

We decided to establish a colony here. On a hill near the mouth of the river we set to work building a settlement. But the Indians, who at first had been friendly, seemed to resent this. We heard reports that they were planning an attack so we retreated to our ships.

I sent Mendez and Perez ashore to discover what the Indians were doing. They soon came across Indians armed with bows and arrows, and had it not been for the quick thinking of Mendez, they probably would have been killed.

Calmly, Mendez sat down on a log and began to

lay out his shaving equipment. Perez put a cloth around Mendez, lathered his face, and proceeded to shave him. The Indians were so fascinated by this that they dropped their bows and arrows and watched in amazement the antics of this barbershop duet! But Mendez kept his eyes open while he was being shaved and observed that the Indians were preparing for battle.

Back on the ship he reported what he had seen. We decided we had better leave. But the water had receded in the narrow bay we were in. The ships could not get out. Finally, the tide began to come in, and we were able, by kedging the ships, to slip over the shoals and out to sea.

Our ships were badly in need of repairs. The deadly shipworm had eaten away at their hulls. One of the ships had to be abandoned at the settlement. Day and night we were forced to pump the water from the ships. Our food supplies were low and the men had only moldy biscuits to eat.

Bartholomew and I discussed the situation one night as we lay at anchor.

"What should we do, Chris?" he asked. "The men are very unhappy. I am afraid we may have another rebellion on our hands."

"There is only one thing we can do," I said. "We must turn back and head for San Domingo. Perhaps there we can find some other ships that will take us home."

By this time my illness had flared up again. I was running a high fever. Most of the time I was forced to stay in bed while Bartholomew directed the fleet.

We were on our way to San Domingo when another stiff gale blew up. This time we were forced to make for the nearest harbor we could find. On June 23, we sailed into a harbor of coves which I called Puerto Bueno (Dry Harbor) on the island of Jamaica.

By now the ships' hulls were completely gone. We were marooned on the island! There was only one thing to do. Mendez had traded with the Indians for one of their canoes. Someone would have to make a trip to San Domingo in that canoe and ask for help.

But San Domingo was nearly five hundred miles away, and to cross those rough seas in a small canoe would be a dangerous mission indeed. Mendez volunteered to make the trip. He started out with six Indians to help him row the boat. Before they could get to the other end of the island however, they were attacked by Indians and forced to return.

Again, Mendez took another group of Indians and set out. This time Bartholomew took some men along the shore to protect them from the Indians. They made it out to sea. We watched the little canoe as it disappeared. We realized that our only hope for rescue was for them to reach San Domingo safely.

Ferdinand and I prayed. We settled down on the ships to wait. Weeks went by, and then months. We still waited but there was no sign of anyone. We began to wonder if Mendez had made it.

Meanwhile, we traded with the Indians for food. Ferdinand spent long hours exploring the beautiful island of Jamaica and writing down in his journal all the things he saw.

My illness grew worse. There were days when the fever made me delirious. Ferdinand told me that I often talked to him about passages in the Bible. Once, I told him the story of Saint Christopher, although I do not remember doing it. There were times when I would call for Felipa while great beads of sweat poured from my body.

There were other days when my fever subsided. On these days I would walk about a bit in my cabin and try to read. But my eyes were dim from the fever. Sometimes I could not see even the book, to say nothing of the print.

Ferdinand often read to me. One day while he was reading to me from the Bible, my mind strayed back to my childhood. I remembered again the promises I had made to God. I thought about my life and for a few moments it flashed across my mind like bright clouds moving swiftly in the sky. I remembered clearly all the places I had been, the discoveries I had made, and the honors God had bestowed upon me. But I felt uneasy. Somehow my life was not complete.

Then suddenly the words Ferdinand was reading spoke to me.

"Read that passage again, Son," I pleaded. Ferdinand repeated the words slowly for me.

" 'His lord said unto him, Well done, thou good and faithful servant: thou hast been faithful over a few things, I will make thee ruler over many things: enter thou into the joy of thy lord' (Matthew 25:21)."

Peace came over my soul. I knew God had spoken to me again and I had no fear of the future. Whatever happened to me now, I was sure it would be the will of the Lord.

"Put those arms down!" I heard the cry from Bartholomew. I rushed on to the deck of the ship to see what was happening. There was general bedlam as a group of our men seemed intent on storming the ship.

"What's going on?" I shouted above the noise.

"Get him back inside, Ferdinand," I heard

Batholomew yell. Ferdinand pushed me back into the cabin just as the men climbed over the rail of the ship.

Then I heard Bartholomew's loud challenge to them. "Take the boats and leave," he shouted. "But do no murder. You will surely be punished for it if you ever do get back to Spain!"

Finally, the noise subsided. Ferdinand told me that a group of about thirty men had rebelled, taken the few canoes we had, and started out for San Domingo.

We were left with no boats, a handful of loyal men, and very little food. But we continued to wait and pray that God might rescue us. Finally, my health improved a little and I was able to move about on the ship.

February 29, 1504 was a leap-year day. I had noticed in a book I had on celestial movements that a full eclipse of the moon would occur that night. I summoned a group of Indian leaders to a meeting aboard the ship.

"My God is angry because we do not have any food," I told them. "He says that unless we get some food He will take your moon away from you."

The Indians laughed a little about this. I could tell they did not believe me. But I waited patiently to see what would happen. That night, the shadows began to move across the full moon. The Indians were terrified. They sent a group of men aboard ship to beg me to ask my God to restore the moon.

"I will see what I can do," I said calmly and retired to my cabin. In a little while, when I knew the eclipse was due to end, I returned.

"My God says He will restore the moon if you promise to bring food," I said.

They promised. From that day on we had plenty of food to eat.

Finally, two ships came from San Domingo to rescue us. Great shouts of joy went up when we sighted the ships. We had been on the island for one year and five days.

We left Jamaica on June 28 and sailed to San Domingo. Ovando, the governor, apologized for the long delay in sending the ships to rescue us. Finally, we were given the same two ships for the long voyage home to Spain. We said good-bye to our friends in Hispaniola and sailed off September 12.

I was saddened by leaving San Domingo. I knew I would never see it again. Like a sparkling gem, it lay there on a tiny island in the sea. A place I had discovered, worked for, and said many prayers over. Now, it was behind me, and I was on my way home again to Spain.

One night when the sea was calm, I stepped out on the deck to catch some air. The moon and the stars were shinning brightly overhead. The sails of the ship flapped gently in the breeze. Suddenly I was aware that someone was with me.

"Father, will you sail again to the New World?" Ferdinand asked softly.

"I don't know, Son," I said sadly.

We stood there for a moment, inhaling the good, clean air of the sea.

I put my arm around Ferdinand. "I don't know if I shall ever sail again," I said. "But you will. You and Uncle Bart, and Diego, and thousands more. Someday the ships in this ocean will be so thick that they'll have to burn lights at night to keep from hitting each other."

"And there'll be lots of people in the New World, too," said Ferdinand. "Not just Indians, but all kinds of people."

The Gospel is for all those people, I thought, and there will have to be many Christ-Bearers to tell them the message of Christ.

"That's right, Ferdinand," I said. "Perhaps someday you will want to live in the New World yourself."

"I would like that more than anything else in the world," said Ferdinand.

"Then if you really want to do it bad enough, Ferdinand," another voice interrupted, "I don't suppose there is anything in the world that can stop you!"

We both turned around to look at Bartholomew in the moonlight. His face beamed with a broad grin as usual.

INDEX

Bibliography

Adult Books

Bradford, Ernle. *Christopher Columbus.* (Illus). Viking Press, 1973.

Cohen, John Michael. *The Four Voyages of Christopher Columbus.* New York, Penguin Books, 1969.

Columbus, Christopher. *Journal of Christopher Columbus (during his first voyage 1492-93) and Documents Relating to the Voyages of John Cabot & Gaspar Corte Real.* Markam, Clements R. (Ed). B. Franklin.

Columbus, Christopher. *Journal of First Voyage to America.* With an introduction by Van Wyck Brooks, Books for Libraries Press, 1971.

Columbus, Christopher. *Writings of Christopher Columbus.* With an introduction by Paul Leicester Ford. New York. C. L. Webster & Co., 1892.

Columbus, Ferdinand. *Life of the Admiral Christopher Columbus by His Son Ferdinand.* Benjamin Keen (Trans). Rutgers University Press, 1959.

Landstrom, Bjorn. *Columbus, The Story of Don Christobal Colon.* New York. The Macmillan Company, 1966.

Madariaga, Salvador de. *Christopher Columbus.* Ungar, 1967.

Morison, Samuel E. *Admiral of the Ocean Sea.* Little (Atlantic Monthly Press), 1942.

Morison, Samuel E. *The Caribbean as Columbus Saw It.* Boston. Little, Brown, 1964.

Morison, Samuel E. *Journals and Other Documents on the Life and Voyages of Christopher Columbus.* Heritage Press, 1963.

Smith, Bradley. *Columbus In the New World.* Doubleday, 1962.

Childrens' Books

Baker, Mrs. Nina (Brown). *The Story of Christopher Columbus.* Grosset, 1952.

Dalgliesh, Alice. *The Columbus Story.* Charles Scribners & Sons, 1955.

Foster, Genevieve. *The World of Columbus and Sons.* Scribners, 1965.

Hogeboom, Amy. *Christopher Columbus and His Brothers.* Lothrop, 1951.

Jordan, Mrs. Charlotte Brewster. *Discovering Christopher Columbus.* The Macmillan Company, 1932.

Morison, Samuel E. *Christopher Columbus, Mariner.* Atlantic Monthly Press, 1955.

McGovern, Ann. *The Story of Christopher Columbus.* Random House, 1962.

Sanderlin, George (Ed). *Across the Ocean Sea.* Harper & Row, 1966.

Syme, Ronald. *Columbus, Finder of the New World.* Morrow, 1952.

SOWER SERIES

ATHLETE
Billy Sunday, Home Run to Heaven
by Robert Allen

BUSINESSMAN
Clinton B. Fisk, Defender of the Downtrodden
by W. F. Pindell

EXPLORERS AND PIONEERS
Christopher Columbus, Adventurer of Faith and Courage
by Bennie Rhodes

HOMEMAKERS
Abigail Adams, First Lady of Faith and Courage
by Evelyn Witter
Susanna Wesley, Mother of John and Charles
by Charles Ludwig

HUMANITARIANS
Jane Addams, Founder of Hull House
by David Collins
Florence Nightingale, God's Servant at the Battlefield
by David Collins
Teresa of Calcutta, Serving the Poorest of the Poor
by D. Jeanene Watson
Clara Barton, God's Soldier of Mercy
by David Collins

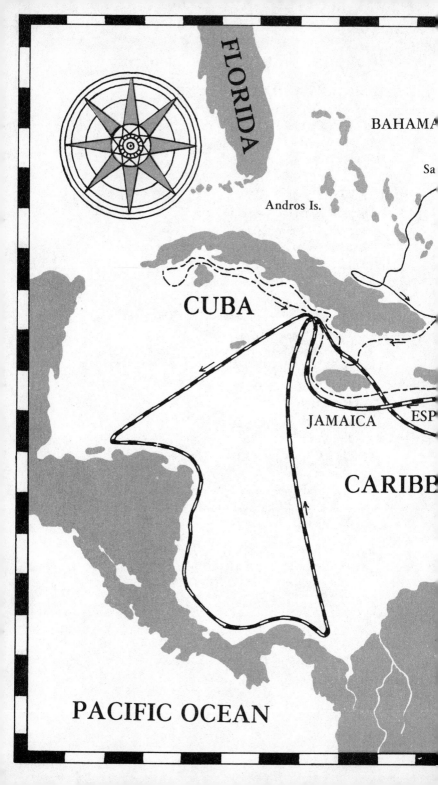

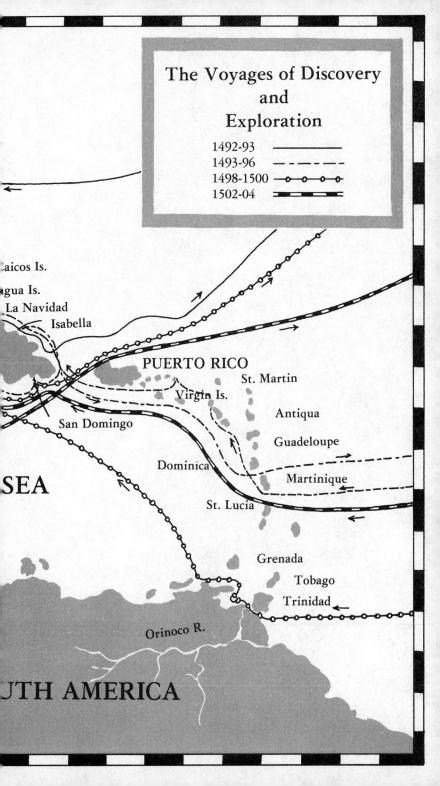

The Voyages of Discovery
and
Exploration

1492-93	———————
1493-96	— · — · —
1498-1500	—o—o—o—
1502-04	▬▬▬▬▬

Caicos Is.

gua Is.

La Navidad

Isabella

PUERTO RICO

St. Martin

Virgin Is.

Antiqua

San Domingo

Guadeloupe

Dominica

Martinique

SEA

St. Lucia

Grenada

Tobago

Trinidad

Orinoco R.

UTH AMERICA